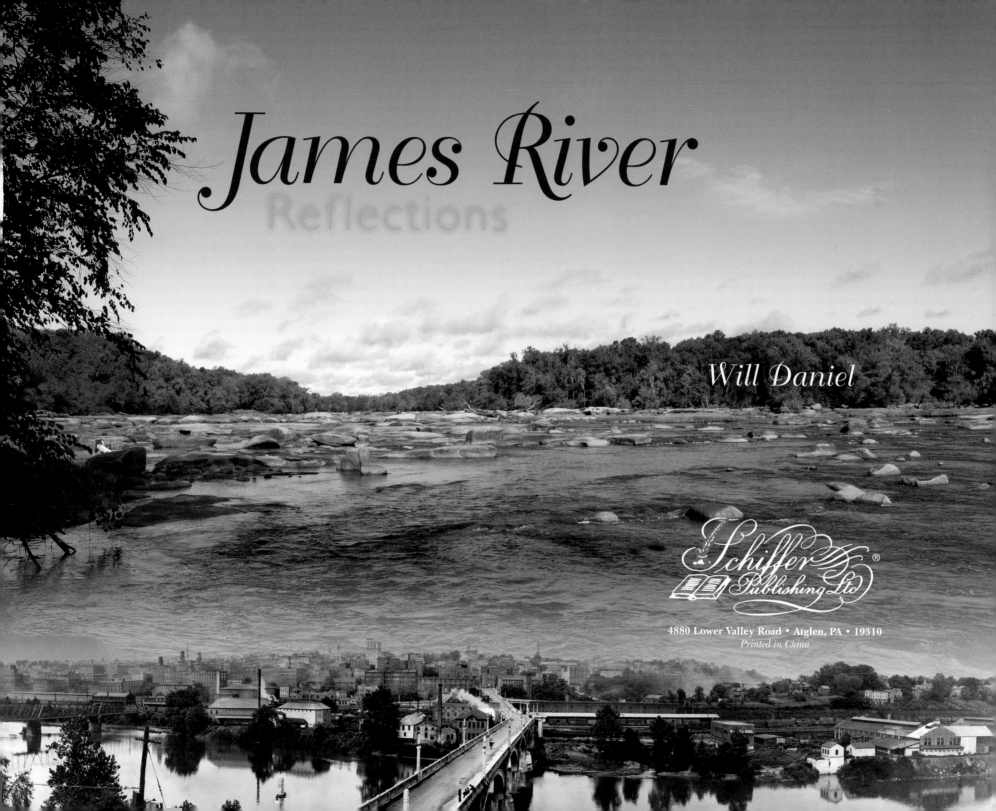

James River

Reflections

Will Daniel

Schiffer
Publishing Ltd

4880 Lower Valley Road • Atglen, PA • 19310
Printed in China

Dedication

For SHARON
Forty-four years together – *Wow!*

Other Schiffer Books on Related Subjects:
Rehoboth Reflections. James Tigner, Jr. ISBN: 9780764331565. $29.99

Copyright © 2011 by Will Daniel
Library of Congress Control Number: 2010943497

Designed by Danielle D. Farmer
Cover Design by Bruce Waters
Type set in Bellevue/Gill Sans/Benguiat Bk BT/New Baskerville BT

ISBN: 978-0-7643-3727-7
Printed in China

Schiffer Books are available at special discounts for bulk purchases for sales promotions or premiums. Special editions, including personalized covers, corporate imprints, and excerpts can be created in large quantities for special needs. For more information contact the publisher:

Published by Schiffer Publishing Ltd.
4880 Lower Valley Road
Atglen, PA 19310
Phone: (610) 593-1777; Fax: (610) 593-2002
E-mail: Info@schifferbooks.com

For the largest selection of fine reference books on this and related subjects, please visit our website at **www.schifferbooks.com**
We are always looking for people to write books on new and related subjects. If you have an idea for a book please contact us at the above address.

This book may be purchased from the publisher.
Include $5.00 for shipping.
Please try your bookstore first.
You may write for a free catalog.

In Europe, Schiffer books are distributed by
Bushwood Books
6 Marksbury Ave.
Kew Gardens
Surrey TW9 4JF England
Phone: 44 (0) 20 8392 8585; Fax: 44 (0) 20 8392 9876
E-mail: info@bushwoodbooks.co.uk
Website: www.bushwoodbooks.co.uk

Contents

Acknowledgments

Charles Gibson, for allowing me access to his private property in order to photograph the head of the James River.

The late Jimmy Dean, country music legend and sausage king, for his words about his love for the river in Chapter Four.

Bill Street, executive director of the James River Association. His expert knowledge of the river helped steer the course of this book. I am humbled by the kind words in his foreword.

Author Ann Woodlief, for giving me words to describe how overwhelming it can be to witness a river's majesty while trying to capture its beauty with a camera.

Tammy Radcliff at Berkeley Plantation for pointing me to the plantation's service road.

Ralph White, manager and senior naturalist of the James River Park System, for allowing me to tap into his wealth of knowledge.

Kevin Costello, Botetourt County tourism coordinator, for explaining in Chapter One the Upper James River Blueway Trail and what it means to tourists and residents.

Kim Payne, Lynchburg's city manager. His enthusiasm for the river is infectious, and his comments in Chapter Two represent a significant contribution.

Charlene Clark, director of marketing at Kingsmill Resort & Spa, Williamsburg, for hooking me up with a golf cart with which to roam the resort and golf links taking photos.

Jennifer Wampler, trails coordinator for Virginia's Department of Conservation and Recreation, for walking me through the plan for the James River Heritage Trail.

David Goode of the Chesterfield County Public Affairs office, for among other things helping me get a boat ride in the James River Advisory Council's 2009 James River Parade of Lights.

Tony Vanderberg, Karen Andruzzi, and Chris and Mary Messenger for graciously accommodating me aboard the *Margo Grey* in the 2009 Parade of Lights.

Army Sergeant First Class Kelly Bridgewater for first accommodating my request for access to Fort Eustis, and later for handling my follow-up requests promptly via e-mail when she was working seven days a week telling the story of earthquake relief efforts in Haiti.

Becky Nix, director of the Lynchburg Regional Convention and Visitors Bureau, for directing me to scenic photo locations in the Lynchburg area.

My daughters, Jennifer Baker and Michelle Garrido, and longtime associates Brett Turner, Ken Yavit, and Susan Barone, proofreaders extraordinaire.

Buddy High, chairman of the James River Batteau Festival, for getting me where I needed to be when I was zooming in on deadline.

Foreword

—BILL STREET
Executive Director, James River Association

Through the prism of history, no single river in America can top the James. The James River is America's Founding River, the front door to a new nation, the path to a new world filled with hopes and dreams.

Of course, the James River is older than America itself. For thousands of years, it served as a source of nourishment and enrichment to numerous tribes of Native Americans who lived along its course. But 400 years ago, the river took on a defining new dimension. In 1607 it delivered a weathered group of Englishmen to its shores, a band of adventurers who built the nation's first permanent settlement at Jamestown.

Since then, the James River has played a central and defining role in the country's growth and character. At first, the river provided the earliest settlers with the basic necessities of life. Later, it became an important artery for commerce, industry, transportation, and even war strategies. Perhaps no other natural feature had more influence on the nation's early history than America's Founding River.

Today, the James River remains critical to our health and well-being. With one-third of Virginia's population living within its 10,000 square-mile basin, the James River touches the lives of more Virginians than any other environmental feature in the state. It is the leading source of drinking water for millions of people. Commerce and industry rely on it daily, as do countless outdoor enthusiasts who paddle its waters, hike its banks or have a secret fishing spot. And the scenic beauty of the river is unmatched. From the Blue Ridge to the Chesapeake, the river is breathtakingly beautiful, enhancing our quality of life and attracting new residents and businesses to the Commonwealth.

As the executive director of the James River Association, I work closely with people who have a personal interest in protecting, preserving, and enjoying the river. The James River Association (JRA) is a private river conservation organization solely dedicated to protecting and restoring America's Founding River since 1976. Through programs of river advocacy, environmental education, watershed restoration, and James Riverkeeper, JRA provides a voice for the river to ensure a healthy and diverse waterway for generations to come.

A paramount goal of JRA is to connect people to the James River and help them understand their own relationship to it. Without those personal connections, that individual motivation to protect the river will be lost. So, while nearly every stretch of the James River has been the backdrop of historic events detailed in text books, it is the personal histories formed each day that are the key to its future.

Will Daniel's tremendous imagery and narrative provide a wonderful and much-needed photographic guide to the river. Despite the river's tremendous history, culture, and natural beauty, to my knowledge this is the first photography book that focuses on the entire 340-mile breadth of the river. Through his masterful photographs and well-crafted prose, Will has succeeded on two levels—capturing the history and aesthetic quality of the river, and enticing readers to create their own chapter of river history.

The book is a perfect companion and promotion for the efforts to establish a recreational water trail extending the length of the river. With the belief that river stewardship comes from meaningful river experiences, JRA together with numerous local, state, and national partners have been working to highlight recreational opportunities on the river, facilitate access, and improve interpretive information. This book's stunning photographs, engaging stories, and fascinating descriptions help convey the tremendous experiences to be had on the river. It simultaneously serves as an advertisement to plant a seed of interest in the uninitiated, as an introduction to the river for those yet to meet its beauty and wonder, and as a journal to rekindle memories of river sojourns past for the river enthusiast.

The health of the James River is a reflection of the cumulative effect of the 2.5 million people that live within its drainage basin. If we are to safeguard this important birthright for our children and future generations, we need to ensure that all of those residents have a personal connection to and appreciation for the river. Will Daniel's book is an important contribution to help communicate the natural, cultural, and historic features of the river and reinforce the wonderful personal histories that are written on James River Reflections.

Introduction

The James River is clear near this bank at Columbia, Virginia. The town is at the confluence of the James and Rivanna rivers, which provide numerous opportunities for recreation and photography.

AMERICA'S FOUNDING RIVER

From Virginia's earliest days, we have relied on the rich resources and enjoyed the natural beauty of the James River. As we grew from that first small colony in Jamestown, the James provided a pathway for settlement and a highway for trade. Today, the James River remains one of Virginia's great natural treasures, encouraging the protection of wildlife and its habitat, and offering ample opportunities for recreation along its banks.

—U.S. Senator Mark R. Warner

The James River is without question the most historic river in the United States. Brave adventurers in 1607 chose a site on the river not far from the Chesapeake Bay to create the first English settlement in America. Farther up river Henricus, or Henrico, in 1611 became the second English settlement in what is now Chesterfield County, not far from Richmond. And, of course, what would Civil War history be without Richmond, the capital of the Confederacy, and City Point, Union General Ulysses S. Grant's outpost on the James at Hopewell? The James River Association, the river's non-profit advocacy group, has adopted the slogan, *America's Founding River*. The well-documented, hard-fought success of the early English settlers along the James is a testament to the importance of this river in American history, and the association's slogan is the perfect way to describe it.

The mere mention of the James River conjures up memorized names, dates, and places from our early childhood study of American history. No one can write a book about the James River without including some of this history. There is just too much of it. However, this is not a history book. This is a look at the river's modern-day beauty through the lens of the digital camera. No film was used for the photographs within this book, other than occasional black and white historical images collected from the Library of Congress. Readers will see spectacular views of secluded places and population centers, and occasionally view comparisons of what it was like in yesteryear.

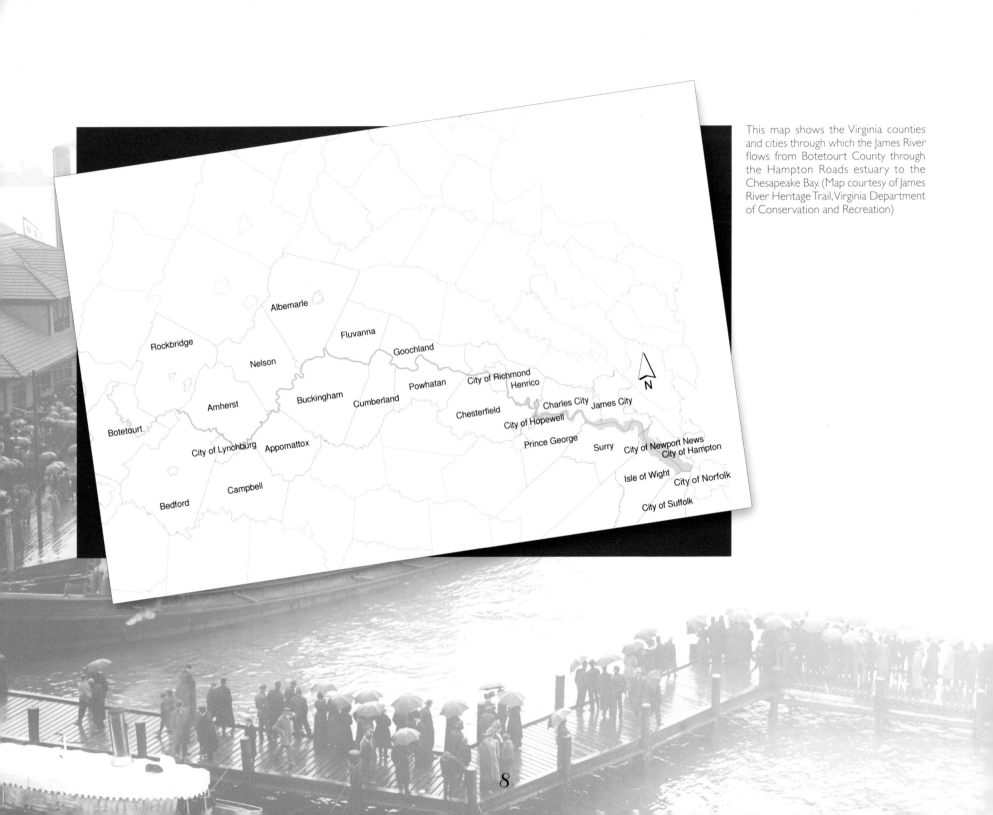

This map shows the Virginia counties and cities through which the James River flows from Botetourt County through the Hampton Roads estuary to the Chesapeake Bay. (Map courtesy of James River Heritage Trail, Virginia Department of Conservation and Recreation)

Where Does the Journey Begin?
Where Does It End?

Because I made it my mission, or quest, to travel the entire length of the James River, I first had to find out exactly where it begins and ends. As simple as that sounds, it isn't. Even though we modern Americans have a 400-year history with this river, publishers of popular literature have a difficult time getting the beginning and end points correct. It's a mystery I had to solve before I could complete my research and photographs. Pick up any reputable book or encyclopedia and it's likely to say the river begins at Iron Gate in Alleghany County. But it really starts a half-mile south in an entirely different county on the private property of brothers Clyde and Charles Gibson.

Trying to pinpoint the end of the river using traditional research sources is even more puzzling. Does the river end where Hampton Roads begins, as some sources state or imply? If so, exactly where is that point? Or does it "flow into" Hampton Roads, as some other books proclaim? So, where precisely does the river end within the Hampton Roads estuary? On the other hand, maybe as some sources state, the river flows "through" Hampton Roads and ends at the Chesapeake Bay, but those sources are vague as to where that point is found. As you can see, the research was frustrating at times, so I turned to the experts at James River Association. The people in that organization are river keepers and environmentalists extraordinaire, and I've come to trust their information about the river. After learning the exact points where the river begins and ends, I realize I could have titled this book *From Charlie Gibson's Farm to Willoughby Split*.

James River Park's Pony Pasture Rapids in Richmond is extremely popular among kayakers and canoeists.

The Journey

When the James River is mentioned people think of Jamestown, Williamsburg, Hampton Roads, Richmond, and Lynchburg. But what about Eagle Rock, Big Island, Bent Creek, Elk Island, Burwell's Bay, or any other of approximately 200 towns, cities, and places of interest that line the river's banks? This book is about those places big and small hugging the river and embracing it. It's about a private patch of land near Iron Gate, a town of less than 400 people that lies about half a mile from the confluence of the Jackson and Cowpasture rivers where the James begins. And it's about a heavily populated Hampton Roads, formerly known as Tidewater area, where the river flows into the Chesapeake Bay carrying ocean-going vessels with it.

In her book *In River Time: The Way of the James*, author Ann Woodlief writes that photographs "fall short of depicting the truth of rivers, for they must halt and distort, especially when they try to capture the river's motion. I know of a few persons who understand this, who have become so entranced with the truths spoken by the river that they abandoned both cameras and language to sit beside the river in silence, day after day" (Woodlief 1985, 4).

I told the author that she now knows one more photographer who understands this phenomenon. It happened to me repeatedly—on Elk Island in Goochland County, at Bailey's Beach in Isle of Wight County, at Osborne Landing in Henrico County, numerous locations in Richmond and Lynchburg, and especially at City Point in Hopewell.

Photographing America's Founding River from beginning to end has been an unforgettable adventure. Finding access points from which to take photographs often involved taking my little car into places where cars weren't designed to go. Thank goodness for four-wheel drive when my grandson Jake and I headed down a dirt road that quickly turned into a pair of deep muddy ruts. I found roads that have state highway numbers on maps, but when I got there were one-lane dirt roads that went on for miles. One particular stretch was nearly ten miles of wilderness so wild I expected to see Davy Crockett or Daniel Boone being chased by a bear at every turn. I found a creaky one-lane wooden bridge at Elk Island, and I kept going because I couldn't stop myself. I met some wonderful people along the way, and I hope to see many of them again.

The Future Journey

Others who wish to take this journey might someday find it easier than I did due to a special project now under way in Virginia. The state's Department of Conservation and Recreation is working on a 340-mile trail system for both banks of America's Founding River from its beginning in Botetourt County to Hampton Roads. The proposed James River Heritage Trail will use river roads and off-road trails that zigzag along the river and cross it in many places to take advantage of historic sites.

Still under development, the James River Heritage Trail is one of five long-distance trail networks in the state that comprise the Virginia Trail Plan, said Jennifer Wampler, trails coordinator for Virginia's Department of Conservation and Recreation. This trail is a result of the increasing interest in river trails nationwide. The first historic water trail was the Captain John Smith Chesapeake National Historic Trail, created in 2007 for the 400th anniversary of the first English settlement in Jamestown. This trail, managed by the National Park Service, has three loops that cover sections of the river from Richmond to Newport News (www.virginia.org/johnsmithtrail).

The James River Heritage Trail is already in use in many parts of the state, but more connection is needed to make it complete on both sides of the river for bicyclists, canoeists, kayakers, horseback riders, fishermen, and hikers. Officials have identified a bike trail along the entire river using existing roads, but only the most advanced bicyclists would feel safe using some portions of it. The state's goal is to make the trail part of a managed corridor for outdoor activities and the conservation of natural resources.

More than four million people live within thirty miles of the trail, representing more than half of the state's population, Wampler said. The trail will pass through farm country, major population centers, and small towns. A forty-eight mile section of the trail is part of the state's Scenic Rivers program, which protects scenic, historic waterways for recreational use by future generations. Many old canals, mills, and remnants of American Indian fishing camps, historic plantations, and Civil War forts are within the corridor, along with natural wildlife areas and parks.

This nineteenth century structure is part of Pumphouse and Three Mile Lock Park on the James River & Kanawha Canal. George Washington was the chief proponent of this canal system in the eighteenth century.

Burwell's Bay is a scenic private James River access point in Isle of Wight County. The site is not far from historic Fort Huger. During the Civil War, the Union Army landed here in 1864 and headed toward Smithfield, but was repelled by Confederate forces.

The James River is home to numerous species of herons and other large birds.

This colorful houseboat can be found on the Amherst County side of the James River on River Road near Madison Heights.

As of early 2010, the Commonwealth of Virginia was seeking private and public partners to develop landings for canoeists and kayakers. The Department of Conservation and Recreation is developing new boat landings at various intervals along the trail. Department officials said the new landings should spur development of campgrounds, bed and breakfasts, outdoor adventure trips, and other entrepreneurial ventures. The plan also calls for improving river road shoulders along the trail, which will require collaborating with public entities.

With Virginia's rich colonial and Civil War history, Department of Conservation and Recreation officials are looking to provide opportunities for tourists and hikers to experience some of that history, while also encouraging outdoor exercise and adventure. To take advantage of historical sites around the state, the finished trail will take a watershed approach instead of following straight along the river. Many existing trails run perpendicular to the river, Wampler said. The state intends to reach out to school groups with an emphasis on interpretation at points along the trail.

Wampler said improvements along the river will provide more venues for community events, historical tours, outdoor adventure games, skill training, and river monitoring and clean-up. She said sport adventure tourism is a fast-growing segment of the tourism industry, and the trail will contribute much to local economies of towns and cities along the river.

Chapter One

The town of Buchanan, nestled between Purgatory and Cove mountains in Botetourt County, Virginia, is home to about twelve hundred people not far from the headwaters of the James River.

GIBSON'S FARM TO LYNCHBURG

Botetourt County

America's Founding River has been called, among other things, the longest river that lies within the borders of just one state. The James River begins at a point in Virginia where the Jackson and Cowpasture rivers come together, and flows approximately 340 miles through the Hampton Roads estuary into the Chesapeake Bay. Many people erroneously believe the starting point is in the town of Iron Gate, population less than 400, in Alleghany County. This is because most popular literature says so. But in fact, the confluence of the Cowpasture, Jackson, and James rivers is about a half mile south of Iron Gate in Botetourt County, and the residents of that county want you to know that. The county was named for Norborne Berkeley, the Baron De Botetourt (Lord Botetourt), who was governor of Virginia in 1770 when the county was created.

This inauspicious spot is the head of the James River where the Cowpasture and Jackson Rivers come together. In this photo, the Jackson River is seen on the left, and the Cowpasture on the right. The property surrounding this confluence is owned by brothers Clyde and Charles Gibson. It was granted to their fifth great-grandfather by the King of England.

The confluence of the three rivers actually occurs on private property. Brothers Charles and Clyde Gibson own the land surrounding the beginning point of the river in Botetourt County. Their family has owned the land for generations, dating back to a grant by the King of England to their fifth-great-grandfather on their mother's side, said Charles Gibson.

Using a satellite imaging program such as Google Earth, one can see at the confluence that the Cowpasture River has a pure, greenish color that contrasts sharply to the brown, muddy appearance of the Jackson River. Where they combine to form the James, the colors remain separated, green on the north side and muddy brown on the south side, for a mile or so downriver until they eventually merge. Charles Gibson attributes the brown color of the Jackson to upriver pollution by paper mills and other industrial properties. The Cowpasture, on the other hand, is pristine by comparison and one of the cleanest rivers in America. In his book, *The Unseen River*, author Garvey Winegar likened the mixing of the colors at this point in the river to "ink dropped into a washing machine." Winegar's book chronicles his 230-mile canoe journey in 1993 down a large portion of the river.

The James winds through the George Washington and Jefferson National Forests, which merged in 1995. The river flows at the edge of the national forest for 64 miles to just below Big Island in Bedford County. Within the national forest is the James River Face Wilderness, which is across the James River from Glasgow. The famous Appalachian Trail goes through eleven miles of the wilderness area.

Botetourt County tourism officials are working on a plan for a system of nature trails to attract more visitors to the river in their area.

"The Upper James River Blueway Trail will provide six public access points in Botetourt County where people can put in boats, kayaks, and canoes," said Kevin Costello, the county's tourism coordinator. "We have already identified three possible locations. We are building kiosks to provide information about where to put in and take out safely. The long-term goal of our water trail committee is conservation and recreation for future generations to enjoy. We are building a Web site where people can become a part of a community. The Web site will tell the story of the river and its watershed to the Chesapeake Bay." The Blueway Trail is part of the James River Heritage Trail, a work in progress by the Virginia Department of Conservation and Recreation.

Glen Wilton

You might have a difficult time finding Glen Wilton
in the U.S. Census Bureau's database, but it is right there
on the James River between Iron Gate and Eagle Rock in
beautiful Botetourt County, and it has a postal ZIP Code.
It also has a bridge that connects Glen Wilton Road on
one side of the river to Main Street, Glen Wilton, and is
one of the most scenic spots on the river. Surrounded by
mountains and national forests, the town's elevation in
the river valley is 1,001 feet.

Eagle Rock

Eagle Rock is yet another picturesque community on
the James River, between Iron Gate and Buchanan. Eagle
Rock was home to several lime kilns that depended heavily
on the river for transportation of its products. The town
was the location of the last lock in the canal system known
as the James River and Kanawha Canal, which was created
by George Washington. The canal was to have joined the
James and Kanawha rivers to provide a transportation
system from western Virginia to the sea. The Kanawha
River is in West Virginia, which was part of Virginia in
Washington's time. Virginia abandoned the canal system
after the railroads made great progress through the
mountainous region.

Washington devoted much of his life to America's expansion, and he was one of the first Virginians to see the importance of the James as a highway into western Virginia. Even before the Revolution, he advocated investing colonial funds in canals to open the upper James for navigation (Rouse 1990, 47).

The 197-mile canal was one of the most ambitious engineering feats in Virginia during the nineteenth century. It ran beside the James River from Richmond to Buchanan. Another section was built to Eagle Rock before the Civil War, floods, and steam locomotives "doomed the concept of a canal system to link the East Coast and the Ohio River system" (Winegar 1993, 11).

Over the years, floods have devastated many towns along the river. The flood of 1985 resulted from six inches of rain in one hour, and wiped out much of the business section of Eagle Rock on Railroad Avenue, including the town's only grocery store and a farm supply store (Firebaugh 2000).

The foot bridge across the James River at Buchanan, Virginia, was built in 1938. Those who are brave enough to walk the bridge are treated to views of Purgatory Mountain (in the background) and the Blue Ridge Mountains in the other direction. The piers of the bridge were built in 1851.

Buchanan

Buchanan, which sits between Purgatory and Cove Mountains in Botetourt County, has the quaintness of small-town America that is difficult to find these days. Artists, tourists, and antique shoppers visit the area. Gallery by the James on Main Street is a cooperative gallery featuring works by artists from throughout the area. Art can be purchased Thursday through Sunday. Also on Main Street is James River Antiques. Shoppers from all over the area visit this store.

About twelve hundred people live in this town that was an important supply depot for the Confederacy during the Civil War. A footbridge across the James River at Buchanan runs parallel to Main Street, and offers views of Purgatory Mountain to the west and the Blue Ridge Mountains

Buchanan attracts artists, antique shoppers, and tourists. This antique shop on Main Street bears the name of America's Founding River.

to the east. The bridge was built in 1938 on piers that were built in 1851. If you're at all squeamish about rickety bridges and heights, don't walk across this one.

"We're just beginning to recognize the assets of the river, especially tourism and the recreational aspects," said Buchanan resident and Botetourt County Supervisor Terry Austin. "In the summertime we now have hundreds of people canoeing and rafting on the river just in Buchanan. We (county supervisors) are thinking more about things we can do to help market the region. We're trying to look at the positive aspects of it, rather than the negatives, like flooding. The flooding is horrible at times, but hasn't been so bad in the last five years. We've focused more on flooding instead of the positive aspects. We're bringing people in from outside the county now to act as guides for canoeists. And we're putting up kiosks along the river banks to let people know of the services available to them."

Austin said the quality of the water in this area has gotten better over the last fifty years. "It's cleaner because the Environmental Protection Agency cracked down on pollution of the Jackson River," he said. "People are conscientious now about keeping the river clean. We all have to live here, so it's in everyone's interest."

Glasgow

Glasgow, with only about a thousand residents and only one and a half square miles in area, sits at the base of the Blue Ridge Mountains. The James River meets the Maury River at Glasgow, in Rockbridge County. The town is just six miles from the Natural Bridge of Virginia, not far from Interstate 81. A massive 1985 flood nearly wiped out Glasgow.

Glasgow was nearly destroyed by a James River flood in 1985. (Aerial photo provided by Town of Glasgow)

21

The footbridge in the center of this photo crosses the James River from near Big Island, Virginia, to the George Washington National Forest (right). Big Island Dam is part of a hydroelectric power station that provides power for about 500 houses in this area.

Big Island

Big Island sits just a mile south of the famous Blue Ridge Parkway, one of the most scenic highways in the United States, in Bedford County. It is home to Big Island Dam, part of Dominion Virginia Power's Cushaw Power Station, which provides hydroelectric power for 500 houses in the area. At Big Island, tourists can cross the river on a footbridge into George Washington National Forest.

This footbridge across the James River at Big Island provides access to George Washington National Forest on the far side in this photo. Some adventurous swimmers dive from the bridge.

The Big Island Dam is a popular recreation on the James River near Big Island and the famous Blue Grass Parkway.

Monacan Recreation Park in Amherst County, Virginia, is just a short drive across the James River from Lynchburg. The Amherst County Department of Parks and Recreation offers various river-related outdoor activities at several points on the river throughout the year.

Monacan Park

This beautiful park at Madison Heights on the James River is named after the Indian tribe that once called the area home. The park includes a boat ramp and small dock, restrooms, picnic pavilion, and play areas for children. The Amherst County Department of Parks and Recreation operates this park, which is just a short drive from Lynchburg. The department offers numerous river-related outdoor programs for children and adults throughout the year.

Chapter Two

A large fountain in the James River at Lynchburg can be seen behind this monument to Confederate soldiers of the Civil War at Monument Terrace on Court Street. At the bottom of the steep terrace is a monument to veterans of World War I.

LYNCHBURG

The large fountain in the James River at Lynchburg is visible throughout most of the downtown area. This is the view from the top of Monument Terrace.

From the top of Monument Terrace to Percival's Island in the middle of the James River, Lynchburg is one of the most charming and beautiful places in Virginia. When I traveled there in the summer of 2009, it was an anniversary of sorts. It had been exactly fifty years since my first and only visit to that city. My father had inherited some land in the area, and I spent some time on the property in 1959 helping him build a shed. I must say the people of Lynchburg are among the friendliest, most helpful people I met anywhere on my journey.

The city is about fifty square miles in area and located near the geographic center of the state on the eastern edge of the Blue Ridge Mountains. For five days in April 1865, the city served as the capital of Virginia between the fall of Richmond and the fall of the Confederacy.

This 1909 panorama of Lynchburg and the James River shows the city to be a well-developed manufacturing center. Foundries, cotton mills, shoe manufacturing, and tobacco drove the city's economy. (Library of Congress)

Attractions

Fine hotels, restaurants, shopping, museums, and art are within walking distance of the river. The Lynchburg Museum is on Court Street at the top of Monument Terrace. The colorful building that houses this museum is a former courthouse that dates to 1855. More information is available at www.lynchburgmuseum.org.

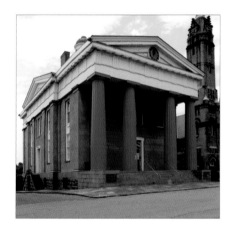

This colorful old courthouse is now the Lynchburg Museum at Monument Terrace in downtown Lynchburg.

Other attractions in Lynchburg include the Legacy Museum of African American History on Monroe Street, the Old City Cemetery on Taylor Street, and Amazement Square, a children's museum near the river on Ninth Street. The city also is home to five colleges and universities, twelve parks, twenty-four playgrounds, and eight community centers.

The James River is rocky at this point off of Mt. Athos Road, Kelly, Virginia (east of Lynchburg).

The monument to Confederate soldiers of the Civil War at Monument Terrace on Court Street is well lighted for excellent night-time viewing from several points in downtown Lynchburg.

Community Market on Main Street in downtown Lynchburg is one of the city's most prominent attractions on summer weekends. Fresh produce and handmade craftwork abound at this market.

The RiverWalk

The RiverWalk at Lynchburg is three and a half miles of paved trail that crosses Percival's Island in the middle of the James River and into Amherst County on the other side, using former railroad bridges at either end of the island. It is part of the Blackwater Creek Natural Area, operated by the Lynchburg Parks and Recreation Department. It is also pure heaven for walkers, joggers, and bicyclists who like their trails level, paved, and mostly shaded.

In 2007, Lynchburg City Council dedicated the footbridge and Percival's Island Overlook as part of the 400th anniversary of the first English settlement at Jamestown and the 250th anniversary of John Lynch's ferry, the beginning of Lynchburg.

Pedestrians and bicyclists enjoy the footbridge over James River at Percival's Island, downtown Lynchburg. The bridge connects Lynchburg with Madison Heights on the Amherst County side of the river.

The James River as seen from the Percival's Island footbridge at Lynchburg.

The James River fountain is a symbol of Lynchburg, and can be seen from most points in the downtown area. This photograph was taken on the U.S. 29 Business bridge (Fifth Street).

The Academy of Fine Arts on Main Street offers art classes, galleries, and wonderful performances. It is located in the 1905 Academy of Music Theatre. At the Renaissance Theatre on Commerce Street, theatergoers have a wide choice of performances, ranging from Shakespeare to Tennessee Williams. The Dance Theatre of Lynchburg offers eclectic performances throughout the year.

Kim Payne, Lynchburg's city manager, says without America's Founding River there would be no Lynchburg.

"Of course, the James (then known as the Fluvanna) River was essential to the founding of Lynchburg," Payne said in 2010. "John Lynch started a ferry here in 1757 to facilitate travel from Albemarle County to the north to New London in Bedford County. Later he had the idea of forming a town on the hill above the ferry site, and a charter was granted in 1786." Lynch was also responsible for the first bridge across the river at Lynchburg, which replaced the ferry in 1812.

This mural on a business wall in downtown Lynchburg points to the James River.

Canoeists and kayakers frequently launch from the landing at this site on the James River at the bottom of Seventh Street. Madison Heights is seen on the other side of the river.

America's Founding River as Transportation and Economic Resource

Payne said the river was a very important transportation corridor for commerce in the first hundred years of Lynchburg. First, batteau boats (or batteaux, plural) transported raw materials, produce, and especially tobacco to Richmond, and brought back finished goods and hard-to-find food products. Later, the James River and Kanawha Canal became the main means of transportation, until replaced by the railroad.

Downtown Lynchburg, as seen from U.S. 29 Business bridge (Fifth Street) across the James River.

America's Founding River at Lynchburg was the site, on June 19, 2010, of the launch of the twenty-fifth annual James River Batteau Festival. More than twenty of the historic replicas, along with countless kayak and canoe escorts, departed Lynchburg for the seven-day, 120-mile sojourn to Maiden's Landing.

The Lynchburg Hillcats (white uniform) hosted the Salem (Virginia) Red Sox at City Stadium, Lynchburg, in a Class A minor-league matchup on July 17, 2009. Salem won the game 8-4.

"Today, the James is a source (although not the primary) of drinking water for Lynchburg and the adjacent counties," Payne said. "It is also the recipient of the region's treated wastewater."

Although there hasn't been a major flood since 1986, many residents still fear the river and look askance at the development that is occurring along the riverfront, Payne said.

Scott's Mill Dam across James River at Lynchburg, photographed from River Road, Madison Heights. The mill has long since ceased to exist on the site, but the dam still provides Lynchburg-area anglers with a great place to fish.

A couple of fishermen try their luck at Scott's Mill Dam on the Madison Heights, Amherst County, side of the James River.

"Lynchburg has rediscovered its waterfront and has made significant investment in a riverfront park and trails system along the river," the city manager said.

"This has been followed by private investment in restaurants, a children's museum, a boutique hotel, loft apartments, and plans for new condominiums."

Although direct economic impact is difficult to quantify, Payne said the river is increasingly seen as a valuable community resource. "About a year ago a float livery was established on the Amherst (County) side, and it provides float trips both above and below the city. Above the dams upstream of Lynchburg is some of the most beautiful river scenery anywhere."

Payne said he has a close personal relationship with the river, spending as much time as he can in a canoe or kayak, or wading and fishing for smallmouth bass. "The river is where I go to unwind. Whether the fish are biting or not, being on the river reinvigorates me."

The Monacan Indian tribe lived in the Lynchburg area until well into the seventeenth century. They were driven out or killed by the Powhatan and Iroquois tribes. Descendants of the Monacan now live across the river in the Bear Mountain area of Amherst County.

The Society of Friends, or Quakers, was the first religious group to settle in Lynchburg. The Friends Meeting House on Fort Avenue was restored and is now part of Quaker Memorial Presbyterian Church.

A footbridge crosses Blackwater Creek in downtown Lynchburg near the James River.

The City of Seven Hills

Lynchburg is known as the City of Seven Hills: College Hill, Garland Hill, Daniel's Hill, Federal Hill, Diamond Hill, White Rock Hill, and Franklin Hill. Point of Honor on Daniel's Hill was the home of the Daniel, Payne, and Owens families, and is said to have been the site of many duels. The home at Point of Honor was built around 1815, and is now part of the Lynchburg Museum System (www.lynchburgva.gov/).

Monument Terrace in Lynchburg includes a monument at the base of the steps that honors Lynchburg's veterans of World War I, and the monument to Confederate soldiers of the Civil War at the top. The colorful building at the top of the terrace is an old courthouse, now the Lynchburg Museum.

Point of Honor at Daniel's Hill in Lynchburg is said to be the site of many duels. This structure was built in 1815, and is now part of the Lynchburg Museum System.

Participants in the twenty-fifth annual James River Batteau Festival prepare their boats on the Amherst County side of the river at Lynchburg. The festival is three days of floating and camping on America's Founding River to call attention to the significance of the batteau to Virginia's transportation history.

Batteau Festival

In the 1800s, long wooden boats variously known as "bateau" (traditional French spelling) or "batteau" (preferred Virginia enthusiast spelling) were propelled by poles up and down the James River, transporting other passengers and goods between Lynchburg and Richmond. The passenger boats were known as "packets" while the poled boats transporting whiskey, tobacco,

Jesse Skillman of Waynesboro, Virginia, steers the **Fluvanna** under a bridge at Lynchburg on June 19, 2010, shortly after the launch of the twenty-fifth annual James River Batteau Festival.

The **Lady's Slipper** has the only all-female crew in the twenty-fifth annual James River Batteau Festival. The annual event is a seven-day float of the historical boats that depart Lynchburg and ends at Maiden's Landing, some 120 miles down river. **Lady's Slipper** has been a part of the event since 1988.

flour, and other trading products were known as "batteaux" (plural spelling). The history of the batteau is so interesting that a James River Batteau Festival is held each year in June, attracting as many as twenty-five of the handmade forty-foot boats to participate in a seven-day float from Lynchburg to Maiden's Landing (www.batteau.org).

The 2010 festival was the twenty-fifth anniversary of the event. More than twenty batteaux launched in this event, with such colorful names as *Lord Chesterfield, Dreaming Creek, Grace of the James, Mighty Joy, Maple Run, Morning Dew, Rockfish Runner,* and with an all-woman crew, *Lady's Slipper.* Adding to the spectacle of these magnificent batteau replicas and their period-costumed crewmembers, a flotilla of hundreds of canoes and kayaks provided escort service from the launch site on Percival's Island.

Crewmembers in period dress navigate the **Virginia Faye** during the twenty-fifth annual James River Batteau Festival, which departed Lynchburg June 19, 2010. The seven-day float down America's Founding River ends at Maiden's Landing.

Buddy High (right), chairman of the James River Batteau Festival, steers his **Brunswick Belle** clear of the bank during the twenty-fifth annual James River Batteau Festival, which starts in Lynchburg and continues for seven days to Maiden's Landing.

Chapter Three

James River State Park in Buckingham County is one of the most scenic spots on the 340-mile river. Fall visitors to the fifteen-hundred-acre park are treated to an explosion of colors.

LYNCHBURG TO RICHMOND

The trip between Lynchburg and Richmond includes this view of the James River as seen from high on Galt's Mill Road between Galt's Mill and Walker's Ford, Virginia.

Bent Creek and James River State Park

The Virginia Department of Conservation and Recreation operates James River State Park, a fifteen-hundred-acre site in the foothills of the Blue Ridge Mountains in Buckingham County, six miles from Bent Creek. It features three miles of shoreline along the James River with beautiful views at every turn. This full-service park includes everything from wheelchair accessible trails to horseback riding, camping, canoeing, and kayaking. The park also has three fishing ponds, fifteen miles of hiking trails, picnic shelters, and numerous cabins and lodges for rent.

The public boat ramp on the James River at Bent Creek offers a myriad of opportunities for water recreation.

Travelers on Virginia Route 605 in Buckingham County will find several spots with spectacular views of the James River like this one near Bent Creek.

Hunter Zaun and sisters Hailey and Madison explore a boat landing at James River State Park in Buckingham County, Virginia. In addition to the river, the park has three fishing ponds and fifteen miles of hiking trails.

The park offers a complete kayak and canoe livery service between the park and various landings. Canoe and kayak rental fees include a return shuttle. The shuttle is also available for a fee to those who bring their own equipment.

Officials at James River State Park in Buckingham County make sure guests are provided with all the information they need to enjoy the river and park safely.

Bent Creek to Scottsville

Between Bent Creek and Scottsville, there are few places with public access to the river, but where they do exist, the views are exhilarating. The James River at Wingina is as lush and beautiful as anywhere along its length. The view from the bridge near the country store there is quite scenic. A similar view of the river can be seen at the Howardsville Trail Bridge near Schuyler.

The Wingina Store and Post Office, Wingina, Virginia, welcomes visitors along the James River.

The James River reflects a bright blue summer sky as seen from the Howardsville Trail Bridge near Schuyler, Virginia.

Opposite: Hatton Ferry near Scottsville, Virginia, is the last remaining poled ferry in the United States. People and cars still ride free across the James River between April and October. It is also the site of James River Runners, a company that specializes in providing rental equipment and excursions on the river.

Recreational opportunities on the James River include inner-tubing using your own or rental equipment. These inner-tubers launched from the landing at Warren Ferry in Albemarle County, Virginia.

These river enthusiasts prepare to launch their inner tubes from the landing at Warren Ferry in Albemarle County, Virginia.

This stretch of the river affords some of the most adventurous aquatic recreation available. River excursions via kayaks, rafts, canoes, and inner tubes take place at various points along this route. James River Runners at Hatton Ferry offers equipment rentals and bus transportation between entry points in this area. On any given day in the summer, hundreds of colorful inner tubes carrying enthusiastic groups of mostly younger patrons depart from the landing at what used to be Warren's Ferry and other points (www.jamesriver.com).

Hatton Ferry

Hatton Ferry is the site of the last remaining poled ferry in the United States. This ferry is still in operation from mid-April through mid-October. People and cars still ride free between Albemarle and Buckingham counties on this historic relic on Saturdays and Sundays from 9:00 a.m. to 5:00 p.m. in season, and if the height of the river permits. A river outfitter's shop is in the old store that was built by the original ferry owner. The store, built in 1882, has been operated as a railroad depot, post office, and general merchandise business. Old canal lock stones, pressed tin walls, and heart pine flooring and countertops are still parts of this historic building. Located within a short drive are Monticello, Ash Lawn, the Blue Ridge Mountains, and The University of Virginia.

The landing at Hatton Ferry near Scottsville in Albemarle County is a favorite launch site for canoeists and other water enthusiasts. The ferry operates on weekends from mid-April to mid-October.

James A. Brown began operating a store and ferry at this site on rented property in the late 1870s. In 1881, he bought the land from S.P. Gantt, at which time the store became a stop on the Richmond and Allegheny Railroad (now CSX). Two years later, Brown was authorized to open a post office in his store, which was named Hatton for the federal postal officer who signed the authorizing statements. Following Brown's death, James B. Tindall purchased the store, ferry, and ferry rights in 1914. He operated the ferry until 1940 when it was taken over by the Virginia Department of Highways.

Hurricane Agnes destroyed the ferry in 1972 and almost ended service. An interested public persuaded authorities to continue this historic ferry, and a new one was built by highway department staff. It was dedicated in September 1973 with the assistance of Richard Thomas, star of the TV series, "The Waltons."

A record flood in 1985 sank the new ferry boat, but the Virginia Department of Transportation replaced it with a metal one launched in June 1986. The operator's building was renovated by the Albemarle County Historical Society to appear as it may have in its early days.

Monacan Indians made their home along the James River banks long before the white man arrived. Indian artifacts may still be found along its shores, including 2,000-year-old arrowheads and pottery. Numerous species of fish and abundant game enabled these Indians to thrive along the banks of America's Founding River (www.thehattonferry.org).

This ferry's days appeared to be numbered in 2010 as the Virginia Department of Transportation threatened to withhold funding for its operation. It got a reprieve in April 2010, however, when ownership transferred to the Albemarle Charlottesville Historical Society. Steven G. Meeks, president of the society, said it is able to operate the ferry as long as riders and concerned citizens continue to support it through donations.

Scottsville

Scottsville is a small town at the apex of an extreme, almost 180-degree bend in the river about halfway between Lynchburg and Richmond. Its location at the bend has been crucial to the town's development over the centuries.

"The James River, historically, has been the 'artery of commerce' in Scottsville," said Brian F. LaFontaine, president of the Scottsville Community Chamber of Commerce. "From the days of batteaux, which moved goods down the river to Richmond, to today's use of the river for leisure, the James has been an integral part of Scottsville's heritage and commerce."

Scottsville is known for tubing, canoeing, and fishing—popular recreational activities at many locations on the river. "These activities draw tens of thousands of people to Scottsville who are seeking the pleasure and fun the river offers," LaFontaine said. "These visitors come off the river in downtown Scottsville and many use the services of our merchants and restaurants. The two river outfitting companies who provide the service of canoeing and tubing along with fishing guides are extremely important to our local economy."

Totier Creek Park, near Scottsville, has more than 200 acres of land and water, including this waterfall area. The park boasts three miles of hiking trails, picnic tables, and restrooms.

Totier Creek Park, near Scottsville, Virginia, includes this canoe landing and fishing pier on the James River.

LaFontaine said the James River in Scottsville is healthy, clean, and mighty. "We are very proud of 'our' river," he said. "Thus, we are always very concerned about anything that could affect the quality of water, fishing and enjoyment of the James."

Scottsville has a history of floods, so the town took action to protect its residents. "The might of the James River is well respected and feared," LaFontaine said. "Flooding in the past caused great damage to our town but a levee built more than a decade ago has tamed the river, and we no longer fear the rising waters."

The Scottsville Museum, at 290 Main Street, offers free admission to learn about canal and river history, the Civil War, and Scottsville's heritage. The museum is open Saturday and Sunday, April through October. The museum is also open for Memorial Day, July Fourth, and Labor Day for special events, and at other times open by appointment.

Canal Basin Square is an outdoor transportation history park at the site of the old James River and Kanawha Canal turning basin at 249 Main Street, across from the Scottsville Museum. It depicts the rich history of batteau and packet boat travel that occurred in the heyday of America's canals.

Rhythm on the River, Scottsville's free summer concert series features a wide range of music styles. Concerts in Dorrier Park are free to the public. Just bring a blanket or chairs, a picnic or order take out in town. Donations to the charitable nonprofit organization keep the concert series going.

The James River, at Scottsville, Virginia, has a history of flooding, but you would never know it from this scenic view. The town built a levee a decade ago to tame the river.

Columbia

Columbia is a quaint little town that sits at the confluence of the James and Rivanna rivers in Fluvanna County, just over the line from Goochland County. It is one of the smallest towns in Virginia, with a reported population less than 100, and a great place for photography. Old buildings, rusting trucks, railroad tracks, and, of course America's Founding River, make for a busy day of photography.

The James River is clear near this bank at Columbia, Virginia. The town is at the confluence of the James and Rivanna rivers, which provide numerous opportunities for recreation and photography.

Crossing into Goochland County on the way to Richmond, we have Elk Island, Pemberton, Cartersville, and Maidens. More than 20,000 people live in this county.

Elk Island

Elk Island is the next stop heading east on Virginia Route 6, and one of the most fascinating places on the journey. The island is three miles from Columbia on Elk Island Road, which becomes a bumpy dirt road. About a half mile south is a creaky old wooden bridge just wide enough for one car and with no side rails. The little wooden bridge crosses the narrow side of the river that was part of the James River and Kanawha Canal.

Elk Island, in Goochland County, Virginia, is a place where photographers can idle away the hours in one of the most peaceful settings anywhere along the James River.

The creaky wooden bridge onto Elk Island in Goochland County, Virginia, is just wide enough for one vehicle.

This is the kind of place where photographers, fishermen, and others simply get lost in time, just sitting there contemplating the universe, the holes in their sneakers, or the stories that one might hear from the abandoned and deteriorating camping trailer if it could talk. A larger bridge that connected the island to Cumberland County on the other side of the river was destroyed in 1863 during the Civil War.

This abandoned, deteriorating camping trailer on Elk Island would probably have many stories to tell, if only it could talk.

Pemberton and Cartersville

A bridge on Cartersville Road, or State Route 45, connects Pemberton in Goochland County with Cartersville in Cumberland County. The views of the river at these towns are mostly like other views along the way, except for the colorful, abandoned bridge almost overgrown with vegetation, parts of which stand on either side of the river as a testament to times gone by. Employees of the U.S. Geological Survey use the remains of the bridge, a curious construction of both iron and wood, on the Pemberton side as a station from which to collect samples for water quality testing.

This unpaved path along the James River bank at Pemberton takes visitors on a peaceful trip through a natural wonderland in Goochland County.

This bicycle apparently took a beating in the James River near Pemberton, Virginia, until it washed up on the bank.

This abandoned bridge section at Cartersville, Virginia, is almost overgrown with vegetation. The bridge is constructed of both wood and iron. A similar bridge section on the other side of the river in Pemberton is used by the U.S. Geological Survey as a station from which to collect samples for water quality testing.

12 FT. 2 IN.

Amy Jensen of the U.S. Geological Survey collects water samples in 2008 on an abandoned James River bridge at Pemberton in order to test the water's quality. Jensen works in the Richmond office of USGS.

Goochland County

Goochland County tourism officials say the James River attracts a large number of recreational users, especially in the summer months, and this is good for the county's economy. The most popular stretch of the river for inner tubing and canoeing is between Cartersville and Westview, although much of the county's riverfront property is blocked by a railroad.

Virginia's Department of Environmental Quality's annual water report said the stretch of river that runs along Goochland County's boundary is no longer listed as impaired for E. coli contamination, said county official Leigh Dunn. That stretch of the river does, however, still contain small amounts of polychlorinated biphenyls (PCBs), said Dunn, of the Goochland Anti-Litter and Recycling Council. Dunn said the small concentration of PCBs in that area does not impact the recreational use of the river, but because they may remain in the sediment at the bottom of the river, they can be found in fish. The source of the PCBs, which haven't been produced since 1977, remains unknown, Dunn said.

Initially known as Maiden's Adventure, the unincorporated town of Maidens was an important stop along the James River and Kanawha Canal, and later the railroad that replaced the canal. The local railway station was renamed "Maidens" sometime after 1888, and that became the town's name. Maidens Landing, a very active boat launch site across the James River in Powhatan County, is now where the annual Batteau Festival ends. A bridge on U.S. Route 522 connects with Beaumont on the other side of the river.

Goochland County resident and journalist Sandie Warwick said she took a trip some years ago on a batteau between Westview and Maidens Landing. James River Association sponsored the trip to generate interest in local leaders to protect the river. "This voyage opened my eyes to the wonder of the James," Warwick said. "This stretch of the river bears little evidence of the intrusion of man. This must have been what the first European settlers saw when they arrived in Virginia. Evidence of man in the form of the spires of Bellemeade in Powhatan and the amazing aqueduct built to carry the canal over a creek was exquisite. The aqueduct, built by unknown but highly skilled stonemasons in the middle of nowhere that few people would ever see, is testament to the philosophy that beauty is its own reward."

Retreating Confederate forces destroyed this mill on the James River and Kanawha Canal above Richmond as the Civil War was coming to an end in 1865. (Library of Congress)

The View That Named The City

The curve of the James River and steep slope on this side are very much like the features of the River Thames in England, at a royal village west of London called Richmond upon Thames.

William Byrd II, an important planter, merchant, politician and writer, was asked by the House of Burgesses to plan a town at the Falls of the James in the early 1730's.

As he had traveled several times to Richmond upon Thames, it is believed that the view led him to name this new town "Richmond."

Dedicated on March 18, 2006 by

Cllr. Robin Jowit
Mayor - Richmond upon Thames

L. Douglas Wilder
Mayor - Richmond, Virginia

Richmond Sister Cities Commission

RICHMOND, CHESTERFIELD COUNTY, AND HENRICO COUNTY

An act establishing the city of Richmond, population 250, was passed by the Virginia General Assembly in May 1742. The city sits on the divide between the Tidewater and Piedmont sections of Virginia, and exists because of the falls of the James River—eight miles of rock outcroppings, small islands, and water vegetation. The river rushes to the fall line where Richmond was built. Below the fall line, it broadens and flows past old plantations toward the Chesapeake Bay (Tyler-McGraw 1994, 1).

This plaque in Richmond's Libby Hill Park tells of how William Byrd II, the city's founder, named the city because of this view that is so similar to one in Richmond upon Thames, England. The Richmond upon Thames photograph on the plaque lets park visitors see the similarity of the two views.

Richmond became the capital of Virginia in 1780. For four bloody years of Civil War, Richmond served as capital of the Confederate States of America. The Confederate government moved its capital from Montgomery, Alabama, to Richmond in 1861 when Virginia joined the secession movement after the Confederate victory at Fort Sumter, Charleston, South Carolina. In early April 1865, with the war all but lost and Union troops advancing on Richmond, Confederate President Jefferson Davis ordered his troops to destroy much of Richmond as the capital moved to Danville, Virginia. Danville was the capital for just a few days. The war was over at that point. Also during that few days in April 1865, Lynchburg served as the capital of Virginia.

Richmond Mayor Dwight C. Jones said in 2010 the river is the city's greatest natural resource and a national treasure. "Running directly through downtown Richmond, the James River is known as the best urban whitewater in the United States," Jones said. "No other city in the United States is able to boast Class IV rapids within its city limits. The James River is truly America's Founding River, with historical prominence tracing back to the early English settlers who explored northwest up the river to what is now the city of Richmond. Today, Virginia's capital city proudly shines as the jewel on the James."

The Canal Walk along the James River and Kanawha Canal in downtown Richmond attracts tourists and residents alike.

Downtown Richmond, the state capital of Virginia, as seen from across the James River in South Richmond.

The Greater Richmond Chamber of Commerce considers the James River an important part of the city's commercial marketplace. "Over the past year, we've seen a renewed interest in the riverfront from local developers, business leaders, and our community, and couldn't be more pleased," said Kim Scheeler, the chamber's president and chief executive officer in 2010. "It's an incredible natural asset to our city and we all need to help support the efforts of those working hard to make it more accessible and enjoyable for everyone."

James River Association

The James River Association (JRA) is a private, non-profit organization whose stated mission is guardianship of the river. According to an independent auditor's report, the organization is funded through contributions and membership dues, grants, special events, and sales of merchandise. Bill Street, James River Association executive director, said the river and its 15,000 miles of tributaries that comprise the watershed supplies drinking water, commerce, and recreation for about one-third of all Virginians, or about 2.5 million people, in thirty-eight counties and twenty-one cities.

A group of concerned citizens established the association in 1976, and it now boasts 3,000 members. "We provide a voice for the river and take action to promote conservation and responsible stewardship of its natural resources," the association states in its mission statement. "We achieve these goals through four core programs: Watershed Restoration; Education and Outreach; River Advocacy; and our Riverkeeper program."

JRA officials advocate for the river on legal and policy issues by serving on legislative advisory boards and lobbying the Virginia General Assembly. JRA's Riverkeeper program employs full-time riverkeepers who monitor the entire length of the river, and its 15,000 miles of tributaries. They are the on-the-water advocates for defense of the environment.

The association has produced water trail guides and maps for the lower and middle James River. They are available for a free download at the JRA website, or you can purchase waterproof versions directly from the association (www.jamesriverassociation.org).

Pony Pasture Rapids, part of the James River Park System in Richmond, attracts more than just kayakers and canoeists. This angler tried his luck on a crisp November day in 2009.

James River Park

Opposite: Pony Pasture Rapids, part of the James River Park System in Richmond, is a Class IV rapids that attracts kayakers from a wide area.

James River Park is a rambling wonderland for water adventurers of all types and ages. According to Ralph White, the park's manager and senior naturalist, James River Park is what separates Richmond from some other cities that have major rivers flowing through them. Some other cities, White said, wall off their rivers, while Richmond embraces the river and promotes it for tourism and recreation. "There are no better Class V rapids in any other U.S. city," for white-water canoeing and kayaking, White said. The rapids are Class IV at normal river levels and Class V at higher levels.

Kayakers enjoy the Hollywood Rapids in the James River at Belle Isle Park, Richmond. This kayaker perfectly performed a roll maneuver when his kayak went under. This sequence took just eight seconds, and the kayaker was underwater for three seconds. The river was nine feet above normal this November day, creating the perfect rapids for avid kayakers.

Opposite: James River Park in downtown Richmond attracts hundreds of thousands of visitors to these rocks every year.

Richmond exists because of the rapids, according to White. The falling water powered all sorts of mills along the banks in the city. Although the mills no longer exist, the river's awesome power adds to the city's aesthetics—its natural beauty. The rapids areas are also responsible for some of the best fishing anywhere in the river, White said, because of a stable substrate and highly oxygenated water. This produces a thin film of fungus and algae, which form the basis of a unique food chain not far from the surface that feeds prize white perch and shad.

James River Park System is the largest park in Richmond. It has eleven parts and more than 550 acres along eight miles of shoreline. A survey conducted by Virginia Commonwealth University in Richmond found that 600,000 people visit the park each year. The park includes islands in the middle of the city and most of the fall line of the James. The park also includes large rock formations, whitewater rapids, and forests. City officials call it "a little bit of wilderness in the heart of the city."

The park offers opportunities for whitewater and flat-water canoeing and kayaking, fishing, hiking, jogging, sunbathing, wildlife exploration, and historical study. A visitor center at the park schedules tours, programs, and activities throughout the year. Volunteers are encouraged to help with nature conservation and resource management projects.

Anyone who has been around the James River for a long time will tell you it wasn't always a beautiful and safe place for recreation. Industrial waste and raw sewage

Hollywood Rapids, named for the famous cemetery on the opposite shore, can be a raging water monster given enough rain. This photograph shot at Belle Isle, Richmond, shows the water at nine feet above its normal level.

This kayaker is making his way through Pony Pasture Rapids, a Class IV rapids that is part of the James River Park System in Richmond.

A kayaker navigates through Pony Pasture Rapids, part of the James River Park System in Richmond.

created stagnant pools and polluted water, particularly in Richmond. However, the U.S. Clean Water Act of 1972 provided the city and state with resources to help remediate the damage. It was a tough anti-pollution law that resulted in a cleaner river. In 1972, the city completed a sewer line and stopped dumping raw sewage. The city also began acquiring land for public use, and the water quality improved dramatically.

In 1981, the park opened the Pony Pasture Rapids section. People who opposed a massive highway project in the area saved this 130-acre plot, once a meadow for horses. It is now one of the most popular places for families to visit. The rocks are accessible by foot from the shoreline and are popular among the city's youth.

In 1982, the park acquired a fourteen-acre plot along the north shore a few blocks east of Maymont Park. This remains the most isolated and natural section of the park system. In 1984, the Huguenot Flatwater was established on both sides of the Huguenot Bridge. This site has steps that provide access to calm water for canoes and kayaks.

Williams Island is just downstream from Huguenot. The island has dams on both sides, and both are owned by the City of Richmond. The North Wing Dam was completed in 1905. The "Z" Dam is on the south side, and so named because of its shape. Both dams provide drinking water to the city. The Z Dam has a thirty-foot notch that was cut into the dam in 1993 in order to facilitate migratory fish passage. Williams Island is a wildlife preserve and has the nest of at least one Bald Eagle. Richmond is the only capital city in the continental United States to have an eagle nesting inside the city limits, according to White. The island is also home to beaver, deer, and other wildlife.

Ancarrow's Landing is at the eastern end of the park, below the fall line. This site has a large concrete ramp that provides access for motorboats. This historic location is the site of the first building and railroad in Richmond, the Confederate Naval Shipyard, and the slave docks where large numbers of enslaved people entered America. The park area includes part of the route slaves walked on their way to and from the docks.

Belle Isle, in the middle of the James River at Richmond, is one of the area's most popular attractions. At various times the island was a Powhatan Indian fishing village, a horse race track in colonial times, a Civil War prison, an iron plant, a rail line, and a steel plant. It is the most popular section of the park. The sixty-five-acre island opened to the public in 1991, when a suspended walkway under the Lee Bridge was finished, linking the island to Tredegar Street on the north shore. Some of the river's fastest rapids flow past the north side of the island, making it a mecca for serious kayakers from all over. The Hollywood Rapids at this point were named for the Hollywood Cemetery, which can be seen on the north shore. That historic cemetery contains the remains of U.S. Presidents James Monroe and John Tyler, Confederate President Jefferson Davis, and numerous other Confederate officials. In addition to the raging Class IV rapids, Belle Isle has a pond in the middle from an abandoned granite quarry, high quarry walls that are excellent for rock climbing, a former hydroelectric plant that operated from 1904 to 1963, and remnants of a water-powered factory. Also on the island are remnants of a notorious Civil War prison and an armor storage shed. Belle Isle was in 1995 listed on the National Register of Historic Places, marking it as a site of national historic significance.

Many Richmonders use this James River walkway to Belle Isle between the historic island and downtown Richmond for their daily lunchtime exercise.

This walkway hanging from the Lee Bridge in Richmond is the pathway for pedestrians and bicyclists to visit historic Belle Isle.

Hikers and bicyclists who use the pedestrian walkway hanging beneath the Lee Bridge in Richmond on their way to Belle Isle are treated to this view of Richmond and an abandoned bridge on the island in the middle of the James River.

Great Shiplock Park, Dock Street, Richmond, is a lock on the old James River and Kanawha canal system that was used for transportation of goods and passengers before railroads put the canal out of business.

Great Shiplock Park is across the river from Ancarrow's Landing. An old canal lock and shipbuilding factory can be seen there. It was built between 1850 and 1854, and it connected the James River with the Richmond Dock at the end of the James River and Kanawha Canal system that went around seven miles of the falls at Richmond. This park is the lowest of the locks in the canal system.

Pumphouse Park along the James River and Kanawha Canal in Richmond was added to the James River Park System in the early 1990s.

The park took over the Three-Mile Locks and Pumphouse Park in the early 1990s. This complex includes the first operating canal system in the United States—opened in 1789 (www.jamesriverpark.org).

Falling water is commonplace along the James River and Kanawha Canal at Pumphouse Park, Richmond. This part of the canal opened in 1789.

This footbridge crosses over a portion of the James River and Kanawha Canal at Pumphouse Park, part of the James River Park System in Richmond.

Activities in the James River Park

Park visitors can choose from a wide variety of activities. From adventurous rock climbing to peaceful nature walks, there is something for every visitor. Whitewater sports include activities such as rafting, canoeing, kayaking, tubing, and swimming.

Art is encouraged on the rocks at Belle Isle, part of the James River Park System in Richmond. This rock is in Hollywood Rapids, near Belle Isle.

The James River Park System in Richmond provides peaceful settings like this one right in the heart of the city.

There's no predicting where artists will display their skills. This log at Hollywood Rapids near Belle Isle, part of the James River Park System in Richmond, was someone's canvas.

Is it a rock or a tree? This tree and rock seem to be one in the James River Park, downtown Richmond.

James River Park Wildlife

The natural areas along the James River provide a sanctuary for a wide variety of wildlife species. Eagles, otters, and osprey are among the oddities for an urban environment. The river has sturgeon over six feet long and blue catfish over fifty pounds in weight. The park is considered a bird watcher's paradise.

An apartment building in South Richmond overlooks the rapids of the James River Park. Richmond is one of the few cities where canoeists and kayakers can experience Class IV rapids within the city limits.

Friends of the James River Park

The mission of the Friends of the James River Park is "to provide an ongoing source of citizen support for the conservation, enhancement, and enjoyment of the James River Parks and their natural and historic environments," according to the park's Web site. The Friends of the James River Park initiated wildlife meadow planting, a regional recycling project with a grant from the Virginia Department of Environmental Quality, and a Missing Link trail project, with grant support from the Virginia Department of Conservation and Recreation. The volunteer organization aided stabilization of historic Pumphouse Park and worked with city government to promote interests of the James River Park System.

An October sunrise prepares to bathe Richmond and the James River in bright sunlight.

December is a holiday season of many lights in downtown Richmond. Light-up occurs around the first of December each year, and the lights stay on throughout the month.

James River Advisory Council

The James River Advisory Council has more than forty members comprised of citizens, governmental bodies, businesses and civic organizations that communicate with public officials about the river. Council officials say their vision is to "unite

Swimmers and sunbathers alike enjoy this section of the James River near a railroad trestle in downtown Richmond.

the community by supporting and promoting the James River as a common resource and preserving its health, beauty, heritage, economic vitality, and recreational value." The organization's volunteers work long hours in the summertime to clean the river's banks (www.jamesriveradvisorycouncil.com).

It's difficult to believe that this section of the James River is in the heart of a capital city. This scene is near the Reedy Creek access point of James River Park at Riverside Drive, Richmond.

Downtown Richmond and the James River as seen from the Lee Bridge, which crosses the river into South Richmond.

Brown's Island is a popular tourist attraction in downtown Richmond. The main river is at the left and what was the James River and Kanawha Canal is at the right of the island.

The pleasure craft *Katie* is decked out December 12, 2009, for the seventeenth annual Parade of Lights. In 2009, thirteen boats sporting colorful Christmas lights paraded up and down the James River in Richmond, and Chesterfield and Henrico County areas to the delight of spectators all along the route.

"The James River is an extraordinary shared resource that has given reason to central Virginia localities to come together to work toward common goals," said Kim Conley, JRAC executive director. "Since 1993, the James River Advisory Council has served as a forum to bring diverse interests and backgrounds to the table to discuss regional issues related to the river and the environment. The James is our region's strongest asset, and the James River Advisory Council is proud of its many members and partners who work tirelessly toward protecting the James while preserving all that it offers our regional community."

The pleasure craft *Katie* is decked out in 2009 for the seventeenth annual Parade of Lights, sponsored by the James River Advisory Council.

A Henrico County Marine Patrol boat monitors traffic on the James River in preparation for the annual Parade of Lights. Local boats adorn Christmas lights in December in a colorful parade up and down the river in Richmond, and Chesterfield and Henrico Counties.

The council sponsors the James River Parade of Lights each December, in which boat owners in the Richmond area dress their boats up in seasonal lights and parade through downtown Richmond, and Chesterfield and Henrico counties. Thanks to the Chesterfield County Public Affairs Office, I was fortunate to ride with the parade grand marshal on the *Margo Grey*, the lead boat in the 2009 parade. That is, the boat started out in the lead until it hit a rather large log in the river, crippling one engine. After that run-in with the log, we limped on one engine into the starting position in fifth place. The *Margo Grey* finished the parade nonetheless and went into the Richmond Yacht Club repair slip at Sailor's Tavern the next day.

Richmond's Founder

William Byrd II inherited vast acreage around the falls of Richmond in 1705. It took him more than twenty-five years, but he finally recognized that the area was naturally well suited for retail trade and a good place for people to live. After Major Mayo laid out the street plan in 1737, Byrd nostalgically named the new town Richmond, because he was reminded of Richmond upon Thames (Woodlief 1985, 84).

This is the view of the James River from Libby Park that prompted William Byrd II, Richmond's founder, to name the city. It reminded him of Richmond upon Thames in England.

According to his journal, William Byrd II was not particularly impressed by the wild beauty of the falls area. He described the roar of the water over the granite as loud enough to drown the sounds of a scolding wife. "His interest in this part of the river was solely practical, not aesthetic, as he figured out how to build canals to his mills and to mine iron ore from the large river island then called Broad Rock. For him the sculptured rock of the James was no more than a nuisance for shipping or a convenience for powering mills" (Woodlief 1985, 85).

This monument to Confederate soldiers and sailors overlooks the James River at Libby Park in Richmond, near the point where William Bird II stood when he decided to name the city after Richmond upon Thames, England.

Tredegar Iron Works and The American Civil War Center

The Tredegar Iron Works, today the site of The American Civil War Center, was founded in 1836. During the Civil War, Tredegar made armor plates for ironclad gunships, including the USS *Merrimack*. By 1863, during the height of the Civil War, more than 2,500 men produced cannons and munitions for the Confederacy at the site. Tredegar also made train wheels and engines, cables, boilers, naval hardware, and brass items.

The center's flagship exhibit, In the Cause of Liberty, presents the story of the Civil War from the viewpoints of the Union, the Confederacy, and African Americans. The center's interpretation traces all three stories (www.tredegar.org).

The American Civil War Museum is a major tourist attraction on Tredegar Street in Richmond, near Brown's Island and Belle Isle in the James River.

The Tredegar Iron Works still stands after much of Richmond had been destroyed by retreating Confederate Troops in April 1865. (Library of Congress)

The American Civil War Museum at the site of the Tredegar Iron Works in Richmond attracts thousands of visitors each year.

Boating and fishing are popular activities in the downtown section of Richmond, the state capital.

Dr. Eugene Maurakis from the University of Richmond uses a backpack electroshocker to momentarily stun fish in July 2009 so visiting high school students from Greece can collect them and evaluate the stream's health. They were testing in Reedy Creek, a James River tributary in downtown Richmond, and comparing the number of species and their abundance to those in forest streams.

A fisherman takes a break at the James River and Kanawha Canal in downtown Richmond.

This view of Richmond and the Manchester Bridge is from the floodwall on the south side of the James River.

Residents of Riverside Drive in Richmond are fortunate to have this view of the James River just west of Pony Pasture Rapids.

Downtown Richmond and Manchester Bridge seen from the south side of America's Founding River.

Brown's Island, a popular tourist attraction, is on the right side of this section of the James River and Kanawha Canal in downtown Richmond.

The James River in downtown Richmond is dotted with numerous small islands like this one. This view is from Brown's Island.

After a heavy rain, the James River raged through Richmond on January 27, 2010, at eighteen feet above its normal level. Local officials report that such levels occur every eight to ten years.

Rapids in the James River at downtown Richmond provide a mecca for kayakers, canoeists, and other river enthusiasts. This view was photographed from Brown's Island, a popular tourist area.

A family of turtles takes a sunbath in this swamp near the James River in Chesterfield County.

The Colonial Dames of America erected this monument in 1910 to commemorate a college that was established in 1619 on this site in what was then Henricopolis. Originally Henricus, it was the second English settlement on the James River, established in 1611. The town was nearly destroyed and most of its residents murdered during a 1622 Indian uprising.

Chesterfield County

Chesterfield County is just downriver from the falls and Richmond. The county is home to America's second English settlement and some historic Civil War sites. James J. L. Stegmaier, county administrator, said America's Founding River is "a vital natural and economic resource to which we owe much of our rich history as a county. The river's importance to Chesterfield County and the region today rivals its role in 1611, when settlers stepped atop a rise overlooking the river near today's Dutch Gap and began new lives and the eventual founding of Chesterfield."

Henricus Historical Park overlooks the James River from high on a bluff at Dutch Gap in Chesterfield County.

The Second English Settlement

Sir Thomas Dale constructed a garrison called Henrico near the site of the Arrohattec Indian village below the falls. The Citie of Henricus Historical Park today sits on the site in Chesterfield County. "Dale's village of Henrico was notable for several reasons," writes author Marie Tyler-McGraw in her book *At the Falls: Richmond, Virginia, and Its People.* "It was here that colonist John Rolfe experimented with varieties of tobacco and where Pocahontas ... was kidnapped and held hostage as a part of the war between the English and Powhatan Indians. The Jamestown settlers were originally instructed to make allies of the Indians, and some efforts to make treaties and to incorporate the two societies had continued despite hostilities. The most dramatic of these efforts was the marriage of Pocahontas to John Rolfe. Having been converted to Christianity while a hostage, she took the English name Rebecca. After her marriage to Rolfe, she bore a son, traveled to England, was presented at the court, and died, as she was about to return to Virginia. The legend of the Indian princess, whose marriage brought a temporary cessation to Anglo-Powhatan wars, became the favorite English symbol of bonding with Virginia" (Tyler-McGraw 1994, 18).

Henricus was mostly destroyed in an Indian uprising in March 1622. Indians burned houses and murdered most of the residents. Survivors of the attack retreated to Jamestown and other settlements, and abandoned Henricus.

Wildlife abounds in this swamp adjacent to the James River near Henricus Historical Park in Chesterfield County.

Drewry's Bluff, one of several Confederate batteries high above the James River in Chesterfield County, prevented Union gunships from attacking Richmond during the Civil War.

Drewry's Bluff

Confederate Captain Augustus Drewry in 1862 built the fort known as both Drewry's Bluff and Fort Darling on a ninety-foot cliff overlooking the James River just below Richmond. On May 13, 1862, Drewry and his troops heard that Union gunboats were on their way. Sharpshooters and riflemen dug in on the banks of the James, and the Washington Artillery from New Orleans entrenched themselves on the opposite bank of the river, providing Confederate artillery fire from the other side of the river.

The three-and-a-half-hour battle of Drewry's Bluff was significant because Confederate troops there were able to successfully repel the Union gunboats, which retreated down the river, preventing a naval offensive against Richmond (Nesbitt 1993, 95).

After the battle of Drewry's Bluff, Confederate soldiers strengthened the fort and made it permanent. For two years after the battle, the fort served as a training site for Confederate Marines. The fort once again defended against a Union naval attack in May 1864, and remained an important part of Richmond's defense until the end of the war.

From this site at Drewry's Bluff in Chesterfield County, Confederate troops successfully defended Richmond against Union gunboat attacks during the Civil War. After the 1862 Battle of Drewry's Bluff, the site was used for training Confederate Marines.

Battery Dantzler

Battery Dantzler was a Confederate fort overlooking the James River at an area known as Trent's Reach. Battery Dantzler and Drewry's Bluff a bit farther upriver both protected Richmond from river assaults by Union gunboats (Nesbitt 1993, 132).

Union General Henry L. Abbot and staff pose for this post-Civil War photo at Drewry's Bluff on the James River at Chesterfield County. During the war, artillery at this site 90 feet above the James River prevented Union ships from attacking Richmond. (Library of Congress)

Confederate Battery Dantzler was one of several batteries located on bluffs high above the James River near Richmond that prevented the Union Navy from attacking the Confederate capital. (Library of Congress)

The view today from the Battery Dantzler Civil War site in Chesterfield County is quite different than it was during the Civil War.

The container vessel *Independent Accord* passes through Dutch Gap in Chesterfield County as it heads up the James River toward the Port of Richmond.

Dutch Gap

Union General Benjamin Butler devised a plan to counter the effectiveness of Battery Dantzler by actually changing the course of the James River. Where the James took a five-mile loop around Farrar's Island, Butler decided to dig a canal across a narrow neck of land, which would avoid Trent's Reach and Battery Dantzler. Construction on the canal that created Dutch Gap began in August 1864, but it wasn't completed until after the Civil War ended (Nesbitt 1993, 133).

The Dutch Gap canal was completed in Chesterfield County in 1865, just as the Civil War was coming to a close. (Library of Congress)

The tugboats *Merrimac* and *Carolina* swap places behind a barge loaded with sand on the James River at Dutch Gap in Chesterfield County.

80

Today, the James River flows through Dutch Gap instead of making the loop around the island. It is the site of one the busiest public boat landings on America's Founding River. "We realize the river's importance through what it continues to provide—commerce, recreation, tourism, inspiration—and we will continue to work with others throughout the region to promote, enhance, and preserve this shining natural feature for years to come," Stegmaier said in April 2010.

Blue herons are a common sight along the James River. This one was found at Osborne Landing, Henrico County.

Members of the Virginia Game and Inland Fisheries Conservation Police force participate in a boat training exercise in June 2009 at Osborne Landing, Henrico County.

Henrico County

Henrico County was settled in 1611, and was one of eight original counties in the new English colony. The county wraps around the city of Richmond, and the James River is its southern boundary east and west of Richmond. Much of Henrico County is along the north shore of the river opposite Chesterfield County. Henricus, the site of the second English settlement in what is now Chesterfield County, was originally part of Henrico County.

"Henrico County was formed in 1611, and we are about to celebrate our 400th anniversary," said Henrico County Manager Virgil R. Hazelett. "The James River brought people to the original location of Henrico County and it has since been a valuable implementation of transportation, tourism, recreation,

and amenity to the lives of our citizens. The river provides a boundary of Henrico County, which in 1611 was extremely large and included Chesterfield County and the City of Richmond. It also provides a scenic relief to the hustle and bustle of other activities in Henrico County and is a constant reminder that nature can change and impact any community in a positive and negative way in a very short period of time."

Hazelett said without the James River, Henrico County would not have grown and would not have developed. The river is the county's major source of water. "Obviously, boating activities, both business and recreation, are located within Henrico County and are routinely used to provide assistance to our citizens," Hazelett said. "The river was the original lifeblood of Henrico County and continues to be a very important factor in our history, growth, development, and future."

Chaffin's Bluff—Historical Site and Luxury Estate

Chaffin's Bluff was a Confederate fort high above the James River during the Civil War. Between that fort and the one a mile away on the other side of the river at Drewry's Bluff, no Union gunships could penetrate Richmond. But today you won't find Chaffin's Bluff on the map. It is the luxury estate of a country music legend whose name is still on the label of the best sausage in America. In late March 2010, just a two and a half months before he passed away, I asked Jimmy Dean why he and his wife, Donna Meade Dean—a Richmond native and also a country music singer—chose this spot on the river after having lived in all those other, glamorous places.

"When we first bought the property, we loved the fact that the James River was navigable all the way to the Atlantic Ocean,

Chaffin's Bluff, once a Confederate fort on the James River in Henrico County, in 1991 became the private estate of the late Jimmy Dean, a country music legend whose name appears on the label of a top-selling sausage brand. The fort at Chaffin's Bluff prevented Union gunships from attacking Richmond during the Civil War. The estate is now Jimmy Dean's final resting place.

Two park visitors and their dogs explore the James River at Osborne Landing, Henrico County.

since we had owned a motor yacht for many years," the native Texan said. "Now we enjoy the river on our pontoon boat."

I asked him what it was about America's Founding River that was so special to him. "The property we own called Chaffin's Bluff on the James River is the place I should have lived all my life," he said. Almost prophetically, he added, "It is the sweetest place on earth to me, and no amount of money could ever buy it. It will in fact be the site of my final resting place with my memorial overlooking the James River." He died June 14, 2010, at the age of 81.

Earlier in 2010, Jimmy Dean was inducted into the national Country Music Hall of Fame. He was previously inducted into the Virginia Country Music Hall of Fame (1997), and the Texas Country Music Hall of Fame (2005).

Virginia Game and Inland Fisheries Conservation Police depart Osborne Landing, Henrico County, to take part in a June 2009 training exercise.

A fisherman relaxes and watches a barge head up the James River at Osborne Landing, Henrico County.

A partially sunken houseboat is tied up near Richmond Yacht Basin, Henrico County.

The park at Osborne Landing, Henrico County, includes this fishing pier on the James River.

Richmond Yacht Basin in Henrico County is the home of several colorful pleasure craft and the starting point for several participants in the annual Parade of Lights in which boats dressed up in Christmas lights parade up and down the James River in the Richmond area.

The *Chesapeake Star* pushes a barge up the James River toward Richmond through Dutch Gap in Chesterfield County.

The mail boat *City of Hudson* is anchored at Jones' Landing on the south shore of the James River in Chesterfield County, c. 1861-1869. (Library of Congress)

The James River Park System in Richmond provides peaceful settings like this one. Capital city buildings are visible in the background.

The Varina Bridge crosses the James River between Henrico and Chesterfield counties on Interstate 295. This photograph was taken from the bluff at Henricus Historical Park in Chesterfield County.

The *Lady Camille* from Portsmouth, Virginia, ties up to the dock at Dutch Gap in Chesterfield County after delivering its barge to a nearby power plant.

A rainy autumn day doesn't stop the tugboat *Labrador Sea* from pushing its barge up the James River toward Richmond.

Small dams in the James River, like this one in downtown Richmond, once provided power for mills in the area. The mills are long gone, but the dams remain as a reminder of historic times and add to the river's aesthetics.

The James River Park System in Richmond provides pastoral settings like this one right in the heart of Virginia's capital city.

A covered railroad bridge led from the south bank of the James River to Belle Isle, where Confederate arms were stored during the Civil War. (Library of Congress)

Residents on Riverside Drive in Richmond have some of the best views of the south shore of the James River.

Some of Richmond's best views of the James River are found on the south shore along Riverside Drive.

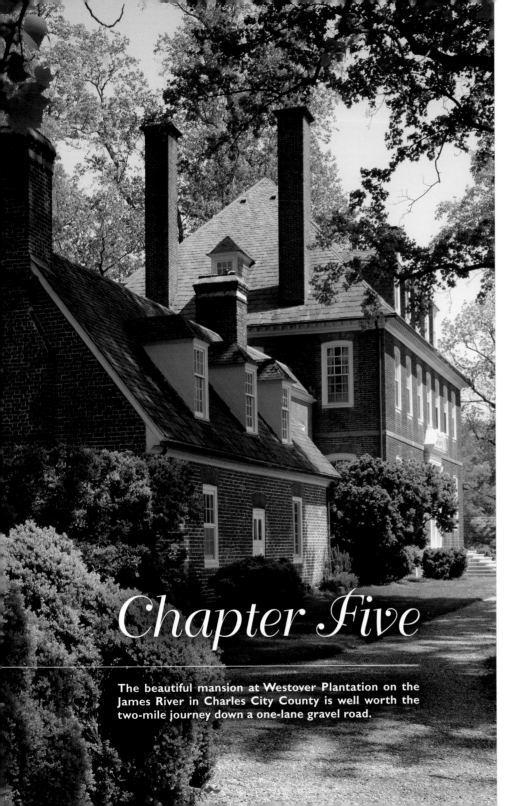

Chapter Five

The beautiful mansion at Westover Plantation on the James River in Charles City County is well worth the two-mile journey down a one-lane gravel road.

HOPEWELL TO JAMESTOWN

City Point

City Point at Hopewell is one of the most important Civil War historical sites on the river. Although not much Civil War action occurred there—only a brief skirmish in May 1862—its strategic location at the confluence of the James and Appomattox rivers made it the ideal location for Union General Ulysses S. Grant to set up headquarters in June 1864 on the lawn of Appomattox Manor. From that point, he launched attacks on Petersburg and Richmond. In August 1864, a barge containing 30,000 artillery shells and 75,000 rounds of small arms ammunition exploded at City Point, killing up to 300 people. Not long before the Civil War ended in 1865, U.S. President Abraham Lincoln spent two weeks at City Point with Grant, General William T. Sherman, and U.S. Navy Admiral David Porter to plan the surrender of Confederate troops.

Union General U.S. Grant's headquarters at City Point at the confluence of the James and Appomattox rivers in Hopewell. Grant's City Point headquarters is a National Park Service site.

After the Battle of Cold Harbor in June 1864, Grant decided to move his headquarters east and south. City Point had already been taken by Union General Benjamin Butler in May of that year, and had a working rail line that ended at the point. In June, Grant directed that all of his troops move to City Point (Nesbitt 1993, 113).

City Point became one of the busiest ports in the world soon after Grant's troops occupied it in 1864. Because Grant chose it as his headquarters, the site became the "nerve center" for the entire Union Army until it broke through the lines around Petersburg, just eight miles away, in April 1865 (Nesbitt 1993, 122).

City Point is considered the oldest continuously occupied English settlement in America. It was established in 1613 by Sir Thomas Dale, and in 1923 was annexed by the city of Hopewell. Before the arrival of the English, the Indians in the area considered the confluence to be an ideal camping ground. Appamatuck, Weyanoke, and Tappahanna tribes had built villages on palisades near the rivers (Calos 1983, 9).

City Point's little-known involvement in the Revolutionary War was brief. British Generals William Phillips and Benedict Arnold, in 1781, marched twenty-five hundred men through City Point on their way to battles in Petersburg and Richmond. The British succeeded at Petersburg, but were defeated at Richmond by the French military leader Marquis de Lafayette (Calos 1983, 11).

Historic City Point, now part of Hopewell, is not as busy a port as it was during the Civil War, but it still handles ocean-going vessels.

City Point historical park in Hopewell is a peaceful site at the confluence of the James and Appomattox rivers. It was here that Union General U.S. Grant set up camp for the Civil War assault on Richmond and the Battle of Petersburg.

When Union General U.S. Grant established his headquarters at City Point, it became one of the busiest ports in the world, handling some fifteen hundred tons of supplies to Union troops. Photograph from the main eastern theater of war, the siege of Petersburg, June 1864 through April 1865. (Library of Congress)

Union Army wagons and transports line up at the wharf at City Point at the confluence of the James and Appomattox rivers. When Union General U.S. Grant set up headquarters at City Point for his siege on Petersburg and Richmond, it became one of the busiest ports in the world. The city of Hopewell annexed City Point in 1928. (Library of Congress)

Shirley Plantation

We've crossed the Benjamin Harrison Bridge from Jordan's Point into Charles City County. Historic Virginia Route 5, also known as the John Tyler Memorial Highway, yields site after site of historical significance. The first is Shirley Plantation, which dates back to 1613, just six years after the English first settled at Jamestown and just two years after the second English settlement at nearby Henricus on the opposite shore of America's Founding River.

The working plantation has been in operation since 1638, making it America's oldest family owned business. The mansion on the plantation, which the family calls the Great House, was completed in 1738 and is in nearly its original condition. Visitors pay a fee to visit the grounds and mansion, and those fees support the ongoing preservation efforts. The plantation is a National Historic Landmark (www.shirleyplantation.com).

Shirley Plantation on the James River in Charles City County dates to 1613, just six years after the English first settled at Jamestown. The working plantation has been in operation since 1638, making it America's oldest family owned business. The mansion on the plantation, which the family calls the Great House, was completed in 1738 and is in nearly its original condition. The pineapple on the roof was a symbol of welcome for river travelers of the day. The plantation is a National Historic Landmark.

Virginia Commonwealth University Rice Center

The VCU Rice Center, formally known as the Virginia Commonwealth University Inger and Walter Rice Center for Environmental Life Sciences, is a 342-acre field station that includes a seventy-acre wetland restoration site in Charles City County. The center is a resource for students, faculty, and researchers to study the ecology of America's Founding River through hands-on experience. The education building on the site was built to the greenest of green standards—the platinum level of the Leadership in Energy and Environmental Design (LEED) green rating system. In February 2010, environmentalists from the center teamed with the James River Association and Luck Stone Corporation to build a 300-foot artificial reef that they hope will restore Atlantic sturgeon to the river. Two thousand cubic yards of donated stone form the reef near the Presquile National Wildlife Refuge in Chesterfield County.

The Walter L. Rice Education Building sits on a bluff overlooking the James River in Charles City County. It is part of Virginia Commonwealth University's Rice Center for education and research, a 342-acre field station on the river that includes a 70-acre wetland restoration site. This building—the greenest of the green—was built to the Leadership in Energy and Environmental Design (LEED) green rating system at the platinum level.

Anglers enjoy fishing in the James River at Lawrence Lewis, Jr. Park in Charles City County.

Lawrence Lewis, Jr. Park

This twenty-four-acre site in Charles City County features a public fishing pier, restrooms, a boardwalk through a swamp, and a wooded trail. Eagles, blue herons, and other water birds reside here. Signs on the property tell of the Union Army crossing the river from the landing at the site. In June 1864, Union General Ulysses S. Grant ordered his Army of the Potomac to cross

During the Civil War, this was the site of Wilcox's Landing. In 1864, Union General Ulysses S. Grant ordered his Union Army troops to cross the James River at this site.

the river at this site and at Weyanoke Point three miles downriver, to Windmill Point on the opposite side. It took three days for thousands of troops, artillery, and supply wagons to cross (www.charlescity.org).

Harrison's Landing/ Berkeley Plantation

Even if you're not a southern plantation fancier, Berkeley Plantation on the James River in Charles City County should be on your list of historic sites to visit. It surely is the most historic plantation in America, and it is conveniently located halfway between Richmond and Williamsburg on Virginia Route 5, the John Tyler Memorial Highway. The highway is named for the tenth U.S. president, whose historic Sherwood Forest Plantation home is just a few miles east of Berkeley Plantation.

Berkley Plantation, overlooking the James River in Charles City County, is perhaps the most historic plantation in America. The first Thanksgiving took place here in 1619, President William Henry Harrison was born here, and the mournful funeral sound of Taps was played here for the first time.

This rustic water fountain is part of the charm of Berkley Plantation in Charles City County. Two famous Harrisons were born here: President William Henry Harrison and Benjamin Harrison V, a signer of the Declaration of Independence.

The gazebo at Berkley Plantation overlooks the James River in Charles City County. The Benjamin Harrison Bridge is visible in the background. Benjamin Harrison V, a signer of the Declaration of Independence, was born on the plantation.

The first Thanksgiving was in December 1619 at Berkeley Plantation, when Captain John Woodlief landed with a crew of thirty-seven men. Woodlief and his men proclaimed that a day would be set aside each year as a holy day of thanksgiving to God for their safe passage from England. This is at odds with many history books, which state that the first Thanksgiving was in 1621 at Plymouth Rock, Massachusetts.

By 1726, the Harrison family had acquired the plantation and built the large, brick house on the site. Among the Harrisons who were born and lived on the plantation were Benjamin Harrison V, a signer of the Declaration of Independence, and William Henry Harrison, the ninth U.S. president. The century

and a quarter of Harrison ownership left its legacy in the name of the landings on the James (Nesbitt 1993, 98).

Taps, the mournful bugle tune played at military funerals, was composed at Harrison's landing in 1862. The site was then Union General George B. McClellan's headquarters and supply base. According to a plaque commemorating the site, Brigadier General Daniel Butterfield in July 1862 called Private Oliver Willcox Norton, his brigade bugler, to his tent. The general whistled the tune and asked the bugler to play it on his bugle. Taps was sounded that day, and has since been played at all military funerals. Also on this site in July 1862, President Abraham Lincoln reviewed 140,000 Union soldiers.

Westover Plantation

This beautiful landmark in Charles City County is well worth the two-mile trip it will take you down a one-lane gravel road off of State Route 5 to get to it. William Byrd II, the founder of the city of Richmond, built the mansion on the grounds sometime around 1730. The house, which is not open to the public, is said to have secret passages built into it. The plantation is named for Henry West, who was the son of Thomas West, governor of Virginia. It is designated as a National Historic Landmark (www.jamesriverplantations.org).

The Byrd family owned the property until 1817. William Byrd I and II are buried on the property. The mansion is one of America's best examples of colonial Georgian architecture. The grounds include 150-year-old tulip poplar trees, formal gardens, outbuildings, and a collection of barns. Three sets of eighteenth century wrought-iron gates are the most ornate in America (www.nps.gov/nr/travel/jamesriver/wes.htm).

A fisherman enjoys his quiet moment on the grounds of Westover Plantation, Charles City County.

These tulip poplar trees on the grounds of Westover Plantation in Charles City County are more than 150 years old.

The beauty of Westover Plantation on the James River in Charles City County is well worth the two-mile journey down a one-lane gravel road visitors must take to get there.

A short drive west on Route 5 is Westover Church, once part of the plantation. It is one of the oldest churches in Virginia, built in 1730, and many prominent Virginians are buried in the cemetery there. Today it is the meeting place of Westover Parish in the Episcopal Diocese of Virginia.

Westover Church, once part of Westover Plantation, is one of the oldest churches on the James River. Actually on Herring Creek, not far from the James in Charles City County, this church was built in 1730, and today is the meeting place of Westover Parish in the Episcopal Diocese of Virginia.

Sherwood Forest Plantation was home to President John Tyler. The plantation on Virginia Route 5, the John Tyler Memorial Highway, boasts the longest frame house in America.

Sherwood Forest Plantation

Sherwood Forest Plantation on Virginia Route 5, the John Tyler Memorial Highway, was the home of President John Tyler. It is about midway between Richmond and Williamsburg. President Tyler lived there from 1842 until he died in 1862. The mansion on the property has a unique and interesting history. Several additions were built onto the main house over the years, and the result is the longest wood frame house in America at over 300 feet.

The house survived a Union Army attack in 1862, and it still bears marks on woodwork and doors. The plantation includes twenty-five acres of gardens and woodlands. More than 80 varieties of ancient trees grow on the property, including nearly thirty that are not indigenous to the United States. One of those is a gingko that Captain Matthew Perry gave Tyler sometime in the 1850s, when he brought them from the Orient to introduce in America.

The Tyler family still owns the plantation, and the president's grandson and his wife still live there. The grounds are open for self-guided tours 9:00 a.m. to 5:00 p.m. daily (www.sherwoodforest.org).

Fort Pocahontas

Fort Pocahontas, or Wilson's Wharf, is near the Sherwood Forest Plantation site on the north shore of the James River between Richmond and Williamsburg. It was an earthen fort built and manned during the Civil War by the United States Colored Troops, and commanded by Union Brigadier General Edward A. Wild. The fort was the site of the "Action at Wilson's Wharf" in May 1864, and part of Major General Benjamin F. Butler's campaign to seize Richmond while Grant attacked from the north. USCT soldiers repulsed seven attacks by eight regiments of veteran Confederate cavalry commanded by Major General Fitzhugh Lee, a nephew of General Robert E. Lee. According to historian Ed Besch, the battle demonstrated that African Americans could fight with bravery against Confederate troops, whose losses were about 175-200 compared to twenty-six casualties for the U.S. Colored Troops.

U.S. Colored Troops seized highpoints along the river at Wilson's Wharf and Fort Powhatan, seven miles upriver, to guard Butler's line of communications with his army. Upon completion of construction, Union troops from Ohio, Pennsylvania, New Hampshire, New Jersey, and New York occupied the fort until it was abandoned in 1865 when the war ended.

Besch's historical research motivated Sherwood Forest Plantation's current owner-in-residence Harrison Tyler to purchase the fort property in 1996 and preserve the historic battle grounds. Tyler is a grandson of President John Tyler, and Sherwood Forest was the tenth president's home. Fort Pocahontas is on the National Register of Historic Places. Civil War re-enactments can be seen at the site each year in the spring (www.fortpocahontas.org).

Fort Pocahontas is near the Sherwood Forest Plantation site on the north shore of the James River between Richmond and Williamsburg in James City County.

Chickahominy River

Just five miles from Jamestown, the historical Chickahominy River flows into the James. Known today for its outstanding supply of largemouth bass and herring, the river is a haven for Virginia anglers. The Virginia Department of Game and Inland Fisheries describes this river as "tidal river fishing at its finest." The Chickahominy is one of the most scenic tributaries of the James, and it played a key role in the survival of Jamestown, according to James River Association officials. The Chickahominy Indians of the area traded corn to the English settlers, keeping them alive during the harsh winters. The Chickahominy tribe today is an active partner with the James River Association in developing the Chesapeake National Historic Trail (www.dgif.virginia.gov).

A U.S. Air Force C-17 fuselage aboard a U.S. Army barge passes by Lawrence Lewis, Jr. Park in Charles City. The Army transported the fuselage to Fort Lee, where it is used for training logistics soldiers.

Chickahominy Riverfront Park in James City County is at the confluence of the Chickahominy and James rivers. The site has a beautiful stand of old cypress trees and is said to offer anglers some of the best fishing in Virginia.

Fort Pocahontas, or Wilson's Wharf, is near the Sherwood Forest Plantation site on the north shore of the James River between Richmond and Williamsburg. It was an earthen fort built and manned during the Civil War by the United States Colored Troops.

The container vessel *Independent Accord* heads up the James River at the confluence of the Appomattox River near Hopewell. The ocean-going vessel was headed for the Port of Richmond.

The Union gunboat *Commodore Perry* and a monitor make their way up the James River during the Civil War, actual location unknown. (Library of Congress)

This view of the James River is from high on a bluff near Jordan's Point, Prince George County.

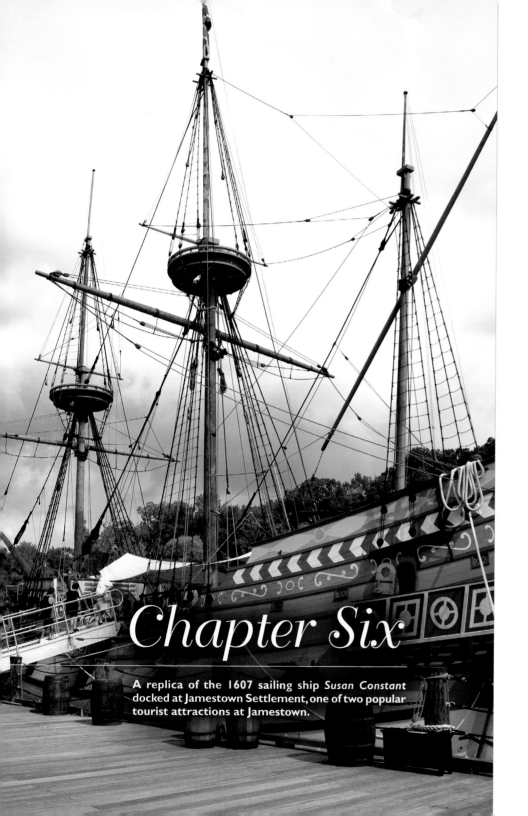

A replica of the 1607 sailing ship *Susan Constant* docked at Jamestown Settlement, one of two popular tourist attractions at Jamestown.

Chapter Six

JAMESTOWN AND WILLIAMSBURG

In 2007, former Vice President Dick Cheney addressed the Virginia General Assembly in Jamestown, Virginia's first capital, and spoke about the 400th anniversary of the first English settlement. "Four hundred years ago today, more than a hundred colonists were a few weeks into their journey across the Atlantic. They were packed in close quarters aboard these three small ships—the *Susan Constant*, the *Godspeed*, and the *Discovery*. Most of us have seen the replicas, and I doubt any of us would want to spend a day in those conditions, much less the months it would take to make that crossing. But they made it—and because they did, the world would never be the same after the fourteenth of May, 1607."

Archaeological digs are a constant undertaking at Historic Jamestown in Colonial National Historical Park. Visitors can watch the digs in progress and view historic artifacts in a museum called an archaearium on the site.

Jamestown

As tourist attractions go, there are actually two Jamestowns. Historic Jamestowne is jointly administered by the Association of Preservation of Virginia Antiquities (Preservation Virginia) and the National Park Service. It is part of the Park Service's Colonial National Historical Park, which includes the site of the famous Revolutionary War battle at Yorktown on the York River. The other Jamestown is Jamestown Settlement, operated by the Jamestown-Yorktown Foundation, a Commonwealth of Virginia agency. Both of these attractions offer historical insights into the first English settlement in America, and both charge for admission.

Tourists from all over the world visit replicas of the 1607 sailing ships docked at Jamestown Settlement. This ship is *Discovery*, one of three that landed at Jamestown in 1607.

At Jamestown Settlement, visitors can see replicas of the James Fort, a Powhatan Indian village, and the three ships that brought the settlers from England: *Susan Constant*, *Godspeed*, and *Discovery*. Visitors can walk on the decks of the ships are learn what it was like to travel across the sea on them in 1607.

Tourists from all over the world visit replicas of the 1607 sailing ships docked at Jamestown Settlement. This ship is *Discovery*, one of three that landed at Jamestown in 1607.

Historic Jamestowne is on James Island. Visitors walk to the settlement site from the visitor center across a specially constructed bridge that offers views of wildlife in its native wetlands habitat. On the other side of the bridge, visitors from all over the world see a plethora of historical replicas and artifacts. Archaeological digs have resulted in the recovery of ancient artifacts from the site, and those artifacts are on display in a museum operated by Preservation Virginia. Archaeologists continue to dig at the site and find new relics all the time.

Visitors to Historic Jamestowne on the James River can see in detail how structures were built on the first English settlement in America, and a sample of the weapons that protected the settlement.

At Historic Jamestowne, even the nails are replicas of the original nails used to construct the first English settlement in America.

109

The church at Historic Jamestowne was built in 1907 and presented to the National Society of Colonial Dames of America as a gift from the Association for the Preservation of Virginia Antiquities. The tower in front of the church, however, is original construction, which dates to 1690. The settlement's first churches were outdoors.

The tower in front of the church at Historic Jamestowne is original construction, which dates to 1690. This is an inside view of the tower.

The Historic Jamestowne site also features a theater in the visitor center; a church, portions of which date to 1690; a statue of the Powhatan Indian princess Pocahontas; a large scale model showing what the site looked like circa 1607-1611; a statue of Captain John Smith, Virginia's first governor, overlooking the James River; and an obelisk built in 1907 for the tercentennial of the English settlement.

The Spanish actually arrived in Virginia long before the first English settlers. The site they chose as their settlement in 1525 may have been the same peninsula

The obelisk at Historic Jamestowne in Colonial National Historical Park was built in 1907 to commemorate the tercentennial of the English landing there.

Captain John Smith, explorer, settler, and first Virginia Governor, is memorialized in this William Couper statue overlooking the James River at Historic Jamestowne. The statue was erected in 1909.

that was to become Jamestown some 82 years later. Spain tried twice to settle Virginia. Lucas Vasquez de Ayllon led the first attempt in 1525. King Carlos I of Spain had authorized Vasquez de Ayllon to settle there. Vasquez de Ayllon described his settlement site as a peninsula, which may have been what the English later called Jamestown. The Spaniards called it "Guandape" and Virginia Indians were still using that name in 1607. A harsh winter in 1526-27 and hostilities with the Indians caused the Spanish in 1527 to return to Cuba (Rouse 1990, 5).

Another Spanish settlement was attempted in Virginia in 1570, when Captain Pedro Menendez de Aviles, Spain's governor of Florida sent a small Jesuit missionary expedition, whose goal was to bring Christianity to the Indians. "The story of the Jesuit settlement called 'Ajacan' was published in 1953 by the Virginia Historical Society in a book titled *The Spanish Jesuit Mission in Virginia, 1570-1572*. The book recounts the sad story of eight Jesuit missionaries and a Spanish boy, Alonso, who debarked near the mouth of College Creek, two miles below Jamestown." The Indians killed the Jesuits, but the boy was later rescued by the Spanish and returned to St. Augustine, Florida (Rouse 1990, 5).

Visitors to Historic Jamestowne in Colonial National Historical Park can view wildlife in a wetlands area as they enter the National Park Service site via a specially constructed walkway.

The Jamestown Ferry approaches the historical site of America's first English settlement on the James River.

International flags and a fountain welcome visitors to Jamestown Settlement, one of two major tourist attractions at the site of the first English settlement in America.

James Island in Colonial National Historical Park at Jamestown features beautiful sandy beaches.

Webb Garrison writes in his book *A Treasury of Virginia Tales*, "Captain John Smith is the sole authority for stories about the first exploit of the girl Matoaka, otherwise known as Pocahontas ('playful one')." She is believed to be the eldest daughter of the chieftain Powhatan, and she appeared to the English to be about ten years old when Smith first saw her. Smith had been captured by Powhatan and was just about to be clubbed to death by his warriors when Pocahontas, according to ancient writings, ran to the spot of the planned execution and placed her head on Smith's, thus preventing his execution (Garrison 1991, 36).

In the winter of 1609-1610, starvation claimed more than four hundred original English settlers, whose numbers dropped from five hundred to sixty. In 1699, colonists moved the capital from Jamestown to nearby Williamsburg.

Jamestown-Scotland Ferry

If you are visiting Jamestown from the South, you might want to experience the Jamestown-Scotland Ferry service across the James River. Virginia's Department of Transportation operates this free service between Jamestown and Scotland in Surry County. Four ferries make up the fleet: the *Pocahontas*, the largest of the fleet, can carry seventy cars; the *Surry* and *Williamsburg* each have a fifty-car capacity; and the *Virginia* can carry twenty-six cars.

A jetty at Black Point on James Island juts into America's Founding River at Colonial National Historical Park.

The Jamestown Ferry boats *Virginia* and *Williamsburg* are docked in the James River at Scotland, Virginia, photographed from aboard the *Surry* pulling away from the landing en route to Jamestown.

The fleet has been operating since 1925 when Albert Jester ran the first sixty-foot ferry named *Captain John Smith*, which had a capacity of sixteen Model-T Fords. The Virginia Department of Transportation assumed control of the ferry service in 1945. Today, 936,000 vehicles a year make the fifteen-minute ferry ride.

Children like to feed the seagulls aboard the Jamestown Ferry boat *Surry* between Jamestown and Scotland, Virginia.

More than 900,000 vehicles a year ride the Jamestown Ferry between Jamestown and Scotland, Virginia.

The Kingsmill Resort & Spa on the James River at Williamsburg features this marina, as well as championship golf, 425 guest rooms, and five restaurants.

Williamsburg

Colonial Williamsburg is the bedrock of eighteenth century American History, and a modern-day mecca for tourists from every corner of the globe. The 301-acre historic area of Williamsburg has more than eighty original eighteenth-century buildings, including the Governor's Palace, from which the British ruled the American colonies. More than four million vacationers a year come to Williamsburg to relax and learn about American history. The town is famous for its artisans such as blacksmiths, saddle makers, and more, who practice more than twenty trades with eighteenth-century methods and tools. Colonial-style shops in the heart of town delight shoppers of all ages and nationalities.

Visitors come from all over the world to see the attractions at Colonial Williamsburg, including a downtown shopping area that showcases colonial goods and architecture.

Kingsmill Resort & Spa, on the James River at Williamsburg, is an Anheuser-Busch property near Busch Gardens with 425 guest rooms and suites, five restaurants, three championship golf courses, and a nine-hole par-three course.

Williamsburg was the capital of the colony and later the state of Virginia from 1699 to 1780, and the second-oldest college in America is located there. The College of William & Mary began in 1693 when King William III and Queen Mary II of England signed the charter for the colony's college. Construction began in 1695.

In addition to historic landmarks, hotels, and fine restaurants, other tourist attractions include Prime Outlets, Busch Gardens Williamsburg, and Water Country USA. Not much of Williamsburg touches the James River, but where it does, there is a world-renowned resort, spa, golf location, and marina. Kingsmill Resort & Spa is an Anheuser-Busch property near Busch Gardens on the James River. The four-diamond resort has 425 guest rooms and suites, five restaurants, three championship golf courses, and a nine-hole par-three course.

Not much of Colonial Williamsburg touches America's Founding River, but where it does Kingsmill Resort & Spa dominates the shoreline. The four-diamond resort has three championship golf courses and a par-three course.

A U.S. Coast Guard vessel comes alongside a Jamestown ferry on the James River near the Historic Jamestowne portion of Colonial National Historical Park.

A replica of a 1607 sailing ship is docked at Jamestown Settlement, in addition to replicas of the three ships that first landed there.

Visitors to Historic Jamestowne in Colonial National Historical Park can view wildlife in a wetlands area as they enter the National Park Service site via a specially constructed walkway.

Artisans demonstrate glass-blowing techniques of the 1600s inside this glasshouse in Colonial National Historical Park. The structure is a replica, and the remnants of the original glasshouse are carefully preserved and on display at the site.

Morning sun makes the James River sparkle near Colonial National Historical Park, Jamestown.

Chapter Seven

Bailey's Beach at Isle of Wight County is home port to several small commercial fishing boats. This small boat did not survive a storm that struck the area.

JAMESTOWN TO NEWPORT NEWS

Geese enjoy the private James River beach at Scotland, Virginia, site of the Jamestown Ferry landing.

Surry County

Surry County, just across the river from Jamestown, was formed from a portion of James City County in 1652. It was named for the English County of Surrey, and included part of James City County that was south of the James River. The Quiyoughcohanock Indians, allies of the Algonquian Powhatan Confederacy, inhabited Surry County when Jamestown settlers visited in 1607. John Rolfe's marriage to Pocahontas in 1614 helped to keep peace between these Indians and English settlers. Scotland, on the James River, is where travellers to Jamestown can catch a free ferry across the river (www.surrycountyva.gov).

Virginia State Police enter a choppy James River at Scotland, Virginia, for search and rescue training. Scotland is the southern boarding point for the Jamestown Ferry.

Chippokes Plantation State Park, on the James River in Surry County, is operated by the Virginia Department of Conservation and Recreation, and the Chippokes Plantation Farm Foundation.

Chippokes Plantation State Park

Chippokes Plantation is a living historical exhibit and one of the oldest working farms in the United States. The plantation's boundaries are the same as they were in the 1600s on the James River in Surry County. The park is operated by the Virginia Department of Conservation and Recreation and the Chippokes Plantation Farm Foundation. The park has traditional park amenities, such as biking trails, swimming, picnic facilities, and a visitor center. Cabins and camping are also available on the site. Visitors can take tours of the mansion, a farm museum, and the plantation fields (www.dcr.virginia.gov).

Fort Eustis

Who knew that the U.S. Army has a fleet of ocean-going ships? One local official refers to it as the "Army's navy." Fort Eustis is home to the U.S. Army Transportation Center, U.S. Army Transportation School, and U.S. Army Transportation Museum. The post's large ships and barges are docked in the James River. I was fortunate to visit Fort Eustis in August 2009 to witness and photograph a special event. Army transportation experts had moved the fuselage of a giant Air Force C-17 Globemaster III transport aircraft from Hawaii aboard the Army ship *SSGT Robert T. Kuroda*. The ship was in port at Fort Eustis

Fort Eustis, home of the U.S. Army Transportation Center, operates river barges and ocean-going vessels from its port on the James River near Newport News.

with the fuselage aboard awaiting its removal to a smaller barge. On the barge, the fuselage traveled up the James River to the Appomattox River, and then to Fort Lee, where the Army now uses it for training exercises.

Today it is known as Fort Eustis, but Mulberry Island in 1918 became the U.S. Army's Balloon Observation School and Coast Artillery Center. Though it had been named by John Smith for its mulberry trees, it was renamed by the Army for General Abram Eustis, a Virginian who had set up the coast artillery school at Fort Monroe in 1824 (Rouse 1990, 153).

Fort Eustis pumps about a billion dollars into the local economy every year, according to the post's 2008 economic impact statement. The work force there includes 12,800 military and civilian employees with a payroll of six hundred million dollars. The fort purchases $277 million in goods and services from local vendors, and twenty-six million dollars in utilities.

Up close, the fuselage of a giant U.S. Air Force C-17 Globemaster III cargo aircraft aboard the U.S. Army ship *SSGT Robert T. Kuroda* at Fort Eustis looks like a whale out of water. The Army moved the fuselage up the James River to Fort Lee, where it is now used for training.

The fuselage of a giant U.S. Air Force C-17 Globemaster III cargo aircraft sits on the U.S. Army ship *SSGT Robert T. Kuroda* in the James River at Fort Eustis. The Army moved the fuselage from Hawaii aboard the cargo ship, and later moved it to a smaller barge for transport up the river to Fort Lee, where it is now used for training.

The James River Reserve Fleet, known locally as the "Ghost Fleet," sits at anchor near Rushmere Shores, Virginia. The U.S. Department of Transportation's Maritime Administration manages the reserve fleet. The U.S. Army's Fort Eustis and James City County are on the other side of the river.

"Ghost Fleet" on the James

I started shooting one July day in 2009 at a place called Burwell's Bay, and then worked my way back up river toward home. At the next stop, Bailey's Beach, I found this marvelous little inlet with lots of commercial fishing boats—small, but commercial nonetheless. In fact, there was a refrigerated truck at the dock waiting for the catch.

While I was there I noticed several huge ships anchored about three or four miles up river. I couldn't get a good shot from Bailey's beach, so I headed toward the fishing boats to ask some fishermen if they knew of a good place on land from which to photograph those ships. I approached two men who were drinking beer on a boat, and one appeared to have reached his limit. I asked them about a good shooting location. The more sober of the two told me to go back out to the main highway, then make the next right, then look for a brand new paved road, turn on that and then take the second or third dirt road, and I would find unsold real estate lots in cul-de-sacs right there on the river bank. Actually, on a cliff right there on the riverbank.

The less sober of the two told me to look out for guys with machine guns. Huh? I just wanted to take photographs. It turns out he was confused about where I wanted to be. I found the

A sandy beach at Rushmere Shores in Isle of Wight County makes a peaceful setting for the fleet of "ghost ships" that sit at anchor in the James River. The U.S. Department of Transportation's Maritime Administration manages the reserve fleet.

place the other fisherman told me about, and his directions were impeccable. I never would have found that location if not for those two fishermen who were enjoying their morning happy hour.

Those "ghost ships" as they are called locally, are the James River Reserve Fleet of merchant ships, managed by the U.S. Department of Transportation's Maritime Administration. When I first got there, I remembered the fisherman talking about the machine guns because a military helicopter came out of nowhere and circled the ships several times. I was sure the helicopter was looking for me.

The fisherman was correct about the machine guns, but not where I was. He was referring to the Hogs Island nuclear power plant, just a short distance from the ghost fleet. Armed guards there wouldn't even let me in the gate. No one takes photos at nuclear power plants, even if they are right there on the river. In fact, the place is blocked out of the Google Earth satellite photo program.

Unsold residential building lots at Rushmere Shores provide a beautiful setting for the James River Reserve Fleet at anchor in the background.

Smithfield and Isle of Wight County

Smithfield is known nationally for two famous products—Smithfield Ham and locally grown peanuts—and the James River was an important transportation route for those commodities for much of the state's history. The river is also an important asset for tourism in the town and Isle of Wight County. "The James River has always been an integral part of bringing visitors to Isle of Wight County—from the earliest settlers to today's recreational boater," said Judy Hare Winslow, director of tourism for both Smithfield and Isle of Wight County.

Smithfield is known for its prized hams, Winslow wrote in her 2000 article "Down Home in Smithfield," for *Cooperative Living Magazine*. "By law, in order to be called a 'Smithfield Ham,' the piece of meat in question must be cured within the town limits of Smithfield."

Historic Fort Huger is on the James River in the northern part of Isle of Wight County, eight miles from downtown Smithfield. Visitors to the fort can view the ghost fleet of merchant ships on the James River, walk the park's trails, and see the cannon mounted along the edges of the fort. Fort Huger is listed on the National Register of Historic Places. The Confederate army built the fort in 1862 for the defense of the James River. The famous ironclad ship USS *Monitor* bombarded the fort that same year, causing it to surrender.

Fishermen unload fresh oysters from the *Lady Nan* on the wharf on the James River at Battery Park, near Smithfield in Isle of Wight County.

Also in Isle of Wight County, Fort Boykin was constructed in 1623 on the James River to protect settlers from Indian and Spanish attacks. The fort was used briefly during the War of 1812 to repel British troops, and again during the Civil War to prevent an invasion of Union troops and vessels. However, the fort fell quickly after being fired upon by the Union ironclad USS *Galena* (www.smithfield-virginia.com).

The commercial fishing boats *Mary E, Nikkie J,* and *Barbara J* dock in this small inlet at Bailey's Beach, Isle of Wight County.

Bailey's Beach

This is one of those "off-the-beaten-path" locations you don't expect to find in your travels. In fact, if I hadn't been searching maps and satellite images for places to photograph America's Founding River, I probably would never have encountered the scenic beauty of Bailey's Beach in Isle of Wight County. It is a little more than two miles off Virginia Route 10, and across the river from Newport News. The sheltered inlet with access to the river is perfect for the small commercial fishing boats that dock there.

The inlet at Bailey's Beach, Isle of Wight County, provides a safe haven for these small commercial fishing vessels.

A fisherman heads to the James River from a small inlet near Bailey's Beach, Isle of Wight County.

Burwell's Bay

Burwell's Bay, also sometimes referred to as Burwell Bay, is just a couple of miles from Rushmere Shores and not far from historic Fort Huger in Isle of Wight County. According to a local historical marker, English settlers arrived in February 1622 at Burwell's Bay on the south shore of the James River in the ship *Sea Flower*. The location, formerly known as Warrosquyoake, was the site of a Union Army landing in 1864 during the Civil War. The 15th Massachusetts Infantry landed there and headed toward Smithfield. However, Confederate forces fired on the Union troops, forcing them to return to their ship (Morrison, www.rootsweb.ancestry.com).

Burwell's Bay in Isle of Wight County is a quiet, private beach on the James River, not far from Rushmere Shores. The James River Reserve Fleet of merchant ships is in the background. The U.S. Army's Fort Eustis is on the other side of the river.

Burwell's Bay was the site of a Union Army landing in 1864 during the Civil War. Today it is a quiet community with a private beach and marina.

Burwell's Bay is a private beach community between Rushmere Shores and Bailey's Beach in Isle of Wight County on the south shore of the James River.

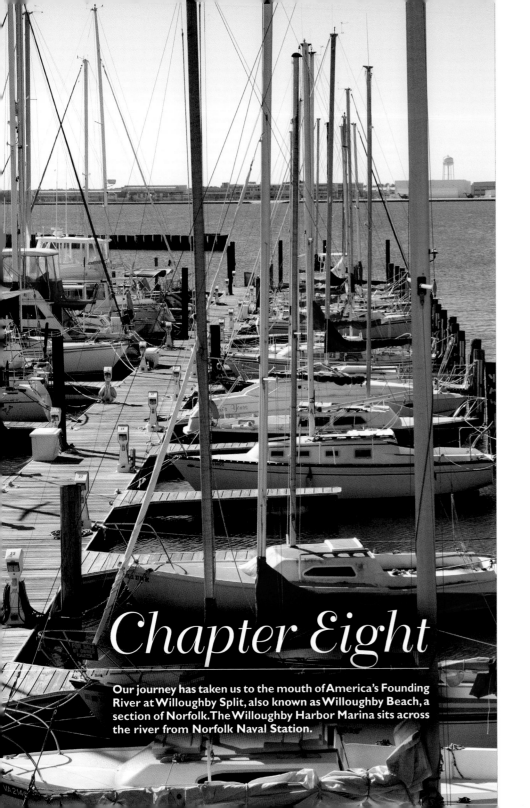

Chapter Eight

Our journey has taken us to the mouth of America's Founding River at Willoughby Split, also known as Willoughby Beach, a section of Norfolk. The Willoughby Harbor Marina sits across the river from Norfolk Naval Station.

HAMPTON ROADS

Wildlife seems to find homes everywhere on the James River. Here, an osprey has nested atop a channel marker in the middle of Hampton Roads.

Just as there is mystery and confusion surrounding the point at which the James River begins, there is miscommunication among popular literature about where it ends. Does it end where Hampton Roads begins, somewhere in the middle of Hampton Roads, or perhaps closer to the Chesapeake Bay? Look at online sites such as Wikipedia, or in various encyclopedias, and you will find assorted vague answers. According to officials at the James River Association, America's Founding River ends just beyond the Hampton Roads Beltway bridge and tunnel on Interstate Highway 64 at a peninsula known as Willoughby Split. The place, also known as Willoughby Beach, is named for Thomas Willoughby, who settled the area in 1610. The British Navy entered Hampton Roads past Willoughby Split in February 1813 to begin a blockade of the Chesapeake Bay during the War of 1812. The British invaded Hampton that year and burned most of it.

The Hampton Monument, overlooking Hampton Roads near the end of the James River, commemorates the 1607 landing of the English colonists.

Willoughby Harbor Marina is in the Willoughby Beach section of Norfolk, where America's Founding River flows into Chesapeake Bay.

U.S. Naval Base Norfolk sits across Hampton Roads from Willoughby Split, the end point of the James river.

In February 1865, President Abraham Lincoln met in Hampton Roads with Confederate Vice President Alexander Stephens in a failed attempt to end the Civil War.

Hampton Roads is by definition an estuary, which is a semi-enclosed coastal area where seawater mixes with fresh water from the river, and the tidal area of the lower part of a river. Estuaries have three main features, all found in Hampton Roads: an open connection with the ocean, an area where salt water and fresh water mix, and a tidal river zone that is mostly fresh water. As ecosystems, estuaries account for about half of the life in the world's oceans. James River Association officials say the entire tidal part of the river is actually an estuary all the way from the falls at Richmond, where freshwater first starts to mix with saltwater, to the Chesapeake Bay.

The river is about three and a half miles wide at this point, with Willoughby Split at the southernmost point and the city of Hampton on the opposite shore. Historic Fort Monroe sits on a peninsula just east of the river's end, in the Chesapeake Bay on the Hampton side. Near the Willoughby Split side is a manmade island built specifically to contain Fort Wool. With Union soldiers manning armed fortresses on both sides of the entrance to Hampton Roads, the harbor was effectively sealed off to Confederate ships during the Civil War.

So we are ending our journey in a heavily populated Hampton Roads, one of the busiest seaports in the United States. The Nansemond and Elizabeth rivers also flow through Hampton Roads on their way to the Chesapeake Bay and the Atlantic Ocean. The Hampton River, located entirely in the city of Hampton, also empties into Hampton Roads. Cities on the banks of America's Founding River in this area are Suffolk, Norfolk, Hampton, and Newport News. Portsmouth, a city of 100,000 people, is not on the James, but is a major part of Hampton Roads and home to a large U.S. Coast Guard facility. Also a city in its own right, Naval Station Norfolk sits right in the middle of this area at Norfolk's Sewell's Point, near the site of the famous *Monitor* and *Merrimac* battle of the Civil War.

Battle of the Ironclads in Hampton Roads

On March 8, 1862, the *Merrimack*, which the Confederates had renamed the *Virginia*, steamed into Hampton Roads and began destroying the Union fleet stationed there to protect Union forts around Hampton Roads. The *Virginia*, more often still called the *Merrimack*, rammed the USS *Cumberland*, then damaged and drove aground the *Congress* and the *Minnesota* (Nesbitt 1993, 82).

Union Navy officers inspect damage to the original USS *Monitor* after her fight with the *Merrimac* at Hampton Roads in 1862. Near the porthole can be seen the dents made by the heavy steel-pointed shot from the guns of the *Merrimac*. (Library of Congress)

The *Virginia's* mission was to knock off the Union gunships. The next day, the ship finished off the *Minnesota* and destroyed other wooden ships guarding the Union forts. That same day, the ironclad USS *Monitor* dropped anchor beside the sunken *Minnesota*. The Union's ironclad had a low profile, making her a small, hard-to-hit target. The ironclad was 172 feet long with a forty-one-foot beam, but its waterline profile, excluding the turret and pilothouse, was only about eighteen inches. The ship needed only ten feet of water beneath its keel to operate. Inside the single revolving turret, the *Monitor* carried two eleven-inch cannons each firing a shot weighing 180 pounds (Nesbitt 1993, 84).

For more than three hours the two ironclads maneuvered about, rammed and blasted one another in Hampton Roads. Troops from nearby Fort Monroe watched, hardly able to see the tiny *Monitor* with its barely visible turret riding a little more than twelve feet above the surface. They knew it would be bad news for them if the ship went down.

"The smaller *Monitor*, with her shallow draft, maneuvered better. White marks had been painted on the deck inside the turret to indicate fore and aft, starboard and port, but the black powder and scuffing of gunners' feet soon caused them to disappear, so the executive officer commanding the gun-crew of the *Monitor* had to constantly call out to ask bearings on the *Virginia*. The *Monitor's* two guns could fire only once every eight minutes, but the Union Ship's high maneuverability made the *Virginia* miss a ramming attempt." The *Monitor* disengaged and retreated, but only temporarily. When it returned to the battle, the *Virginia* also had withdrawn (Nesbitt 1993, 85).

Historians call the battle a draw. But strategically, Union forces won because they gained control of the James River, which they desperately needed. As long as the *Monitor* remained in Hampton Roads, the Confederates could not use the river to supply their armies. Even worse, they could not deny the river's use to Union ships as long as the *Monitor* held the *Virginia* in stalemate (Nesbitt 1993, 86).

Norfolk

The harbor cruise boat *Victory Rover* cruises past U.S. Navy ships in port at Naval Station Norfolk on the James River.

A crowd waits to board an excursion fleet and other ships at Hampton Roads on a foggy February 22, 1909. (Library of Congress)

Norfolk is a city of some 239,000 residents that encompasses sixty-six square miles. Norfolk's mayor said the city's residents appreciate the central role the James has played in Virginia's history as the primary highway to the west and its role in the state's maritime tradition. "For centuries the James River has been instrumental to the Hampton Roads economy," said Norfolk Mayor Paul D. Fraim in 2010. He said the river has traditionally provided jobs to local watermen. "Since the colonial era, it has served as an access point for exporting agricultural products and importing foreign goods. In more recent times it has provided innumerable jobs through the shipbuilding activities along its shoreline. Finally, along with the Elizabeth and Nansemond rivers, it forms Hampton Roads, the largest protected harbor in the world and home to the largest United States Naval Base, and one of the busiest ports on the East Coast."

The city is home of the USS *Wisconsin* battleship and a booming cruise port. Ocean-going cruise vessels of up to 3,000 passengers regularly stop at the pier downtown. Norfolk is home to the Virginia Opera, the Virginia Stage Company, the Virginia Symphony, and the Norfolk Botanical Garden. Old Dominion University, Norfolk State University, and a downtown campus of Tidewater Community College are located in town.

On January 1, 1776, Lord Dunmore and his British ships fired on Norfolk's waterfront and burned much of the city. In 1855, nearly a third of Norfolk's population died in a yellow fever epidemic (Nesbitt 1993, 86).

At the start of the Civil War in April 1861, Union forces abandoned Norfolk and tried to burn everything of military value at the Navy yard there. Union troops retook the city in May 1861 (Nesbitt 1993, 87).

James Adams' Floating Theatre, a two-story houseboat on a barge, frequently tied up at Norfolk and several other Hampton Roads towns in the 1920s. People from all around the area would see such plays as *Show Boat*, *The Balloon Girl*, *Pollyanna*, *Tempest and Sunshine*, and *A Thief in the Night* (Rouse 1990, 186).

Norfolk Police patrol Hampton Roads near U.S. Navy ships in port. The aircraft carrier is the USS *George H.W. Bush*, the Navy's newest nuclear-powered carrier.

The nuclear-powered aircraft carrier USS *Harry S. Truman* is home-ported at Naval Station Norfolk on the James River.

Naval Station Norfolk

Navy Norfolk, as it's been known over the years, is home to the world's largest concentration of U.S. Naval forces. It has been operating and growing since 1917, when the Navy established an airfield for seaplanes there. Today, the base supports the U.S. Atlantic Fleet and U.S. Atlantic Command, both of which are headquartered there. The Navy's 2nd Fleet, one of four numbered naval fleets, is based there as well as a major anti-submarine strike force. Navy Norfolk is homeport to nearly 82,000 sailors and more than eighty ships. One ship, the giant Nimitz-class nuclear aircraft carrier USS *Carl Vinson*, is home-ported across the river in Newport News.

The Navy also employs nearly 32,000 civilians who live in the area, for a combined total (military and civilian) payroll of more than $7.6 billion; it is the city's largest employer. The total economic impact of Navy Norfolk on the Hampton Roads area was estimated by the Navy to be $14.6 billion in 2008.

Across the river in Newport News is Northrop Grumman Shipbuilding, which constructs huge vessels for the Navy.

The Navy frigate USS *Carr* (52) is home-ported at Naval Station Norfolk in the James River. Behind the *Carr* is the guided missile cruiser USS *Leyte Gulf* (55).

The 4.5-mile James River Bridge connects Newport News (foreground) with Isle of Wight County on the other side. The four-lane bridge carries 30,000 vehicles a day across the river.

Northrop Grumman operates one of the largest shipbuilding sites in the world at Newport News on the James River, and is one of the area's largest employers.

The USS *Pennsylvania* launches into the James River in March 1915 at the Newport News Shipbuilding site. The ship served in World War II and was sunk in 1946 when used as a target ship for the Bikini atoll atom bomb tests. (Library of Congress)

The sandy beach at Huntington Park in Newport News attracts large crowds of bathers in the summertime.

Newport News

No one knows exactly how the river's mouth got the name Newport News Point. It was called Newport's News until the 1900s. Captain Christopher Newport, who captained the ship *Susan Constant* on its historic mission to settle Jamestown, made several trips to Jamestown between 1607 and 1611, bringing news and supplies from England. The "news" of Newport's trips in and out of the area may have been responsible for the name (Rouse 1990, 13).

Newport, a one-armed veteran of English wars in the West Indies, in May 1607 led twenty-three men, including Capt. John Smith, upriver toward the falls at Richmond. The rest of the Englishmen stayed behind in the settlement to build defenses and plant corn. The Powhatan Indians watched the men rowing upstream. Local chiefs greeted them each time they landed, and the queen of the Appamatuck met them on the riverbank (Tyler-McGraw 1994, 9).

Near the end of his term in 2010, Newport News Mayor Joe S. Frank provided his insight into what the river means to the citizens of Newport News.

"When the English colonists first entered Chesapeake Bay, they passed the point at Newport News on their way to creating the first permanent English-speaking settlement in the New World at Jamestown," Frank said. "Since that time, the James River has been the catalyst for what Newport News has become as a modern city.

Frank listed some of the historical people and events allowing Newport News to grow and prosper over countless generations. Those included the first military-armed presence of lookouts and scouts from Jamestown scanning the harbor entrance for Spanish raiders, a cluster of houses for farmers and fishermen, and Collis P. Huntington's vision of Newport News as a deep water port to export coal over his rail lines from the mountains of Virginia and West Virginia. Huntington's shipyard at Newport News first repaired, then later built ships that brought national and international commerce to the shores of the James River and Hampton Roads.

In discussing the river's impact on the local economy, Frank said America's Founding River has sustained the seafood industry since the earliest days of settlement, and it continues to thrive there. "But the economic engines which drive the local economy are the ports, shipbuilding and ship repair facilities, and the military." He said one of the main attributes of the Army at Fort Eustis is its access to the James to support its sea-going vessels for worldwide delivery of military logistics.

"The Newport News marine terminal gives the Ports of Virginia the capacity to handle significant quantities of break-bulk cargo that is otherwise inaccessible to other components of those ports," Frank continued. "Northrop Grumman Shipbuilding Newport News… has a significant impact on the local economy not only as a major employer in Hampton Roads but also through the use of local contractors and suppliers, support of our community, and the sailors stationed here as the shipyard builds and repairs nuclear powered ships in defense of this country."

The former mayor said the river's health has been a serious concern since its pristine origins when English settlers landed. "As with the Chesapeake Bay, of which the James is a significant tributary, the river's general health fairly thrived until the kepone pesticide contamination disaster in the mid-1970s (which closed the river to fishing and swimming until 1989) to more modern industrial, agricultural, and residential pollution, restoring the health of the river has been a major challenge for generations. Fortunately, however, with the promulgation of the Chesapeake Bay Preservation Act, voluntary and regulated environmental protection measures and clean up, the river is re-emerging in a promising and positive way. But clearly, challenges remain to restore it and to sustain its health through conservation and regulatory measures."

Huntington Park on the James River at Newport News offers a sandy beach for swimming with lifeguards on duty. A beach food concession is open in the summer, and a boat landing allows access to the river for boats up to thirty feet long. The park also includes a large playground area and twenty lighted tennis courts. The Virginia War Museum also is located in the park. Huntington Park sits at the base of the northern entrance to the James River Bridge on U.S. Route 17. This nearly five-mile span was the engineering marvel of its time when it opened in November 1928.

Hampton

The city of Hampton, with a population of more than 145,000 people, has more than twenty parks, trails, and nature preserves. The Virginia Air & Space Center at Hampton is a world-class museum of aviation history. The Hampton Coliseum, Hampton Roads Convention Center, Charles H. Taylor Arts Center, and American Theatre offer sophisticated culture and entertainment for every taste (www.hampton.va.us).

A 2009 study by the Virginia Institute of Marine Science estimates that boaters using Hampton marinas contribute fifty-five million dollars a year to the city's economy. Approximately eighteen hundred boats are

Hampton is the last city on America's Founding River. This marina in downtown Hampton contains some of the eighteen hundred pleasure craft that are docked in the city. The Virginia Air & Space Museum is adjacent to this marina, which is on the Hampton River, not far from the James and Hampton Roads

docked in the city's marinas, according to the study, which was commissioned by Hampton city officials. The officials plan to use the study to decide tax policies for recreational boats (www.vims.edu).

Visitors to Hampton will find many attractions to keep them busy, including the Riverside Imax Theatre, tour and charter boats *Miss Hampton II* and *The Ocean Eagle*, Virginia Air & Space Museum, Hampton University Museum, Hampton History Museum, Charles H. Taylor Arts Center, Blue Skies Gallery, Art by Gerome Galleria, and The American Theatre. More information about these and other attractions can be found at www.downtownhampton.com.

Chapter Nine

For a dramatic effect, don't be afraid to climb on large objects and shoot with a wide-angle lens. Here, the author is shooting down the barrel of a Civil War cannon at Drewry's Bluff in Chesterfield County, Virginia. (Photo by Jake Baker)

Landscape photography is one of the most popular areas that photographers pursue, especially in the early stages of their photography. Some of the most beautiful images embedded in our collective memory are landscapes, and many of those are of rivers. Every photographer wants to make beautiful images, and landscapes are easier than "people" pictures because the landscape doesn't move; it doesn't smile or frown. Rivers are popular subjects because they are everywhere. Finding access points from which to photograph rivers near you is probably easy. Drive a mile or two and you're there. Everyone has a river near them because rivers were the backbone of early American transportation.

Equipment

If you're a professional photographer you might say you need a large view camera, a rock-solid tripod, and all sorts of special filters so you can get exactly the right effect. You might say you need a great deal of patience in order to stay in one spot for hours waiting for the light to be perfect for that shot you've planned. These professionals are correct—if they earn their living making spectacular landscape photographs.

But what about the rest of us? What equipment would you need to go out today and take wonderful images of your favorite river or other landscape scene? First, let's not get into film. In 2011 when this book was published, digital imagery had made such great strides in quality, accessibility, and affordability that most photographers had abandoned film altogether or made it their secondary means of capturing images. This is not to launch a film-versus-digital argument, but rather to acknowledge the state of the photographic industry and, more importantly, the preference of its customer base in 2011.

So, you need a digital camera. Does it need to be a digital single lens reflex (DSLR)? Not necessarily, but most photographers find the DSLR to be the most flexible of digital cameras. Some photographers favor the so-called point-and-shoot (P&S) cameras—those that have a built-in zoom lens but no interchangeable lens capability. Many P&S cameras include professional features such as raw image processing and large megapixel specifications that enable their owners to make wonderful images suitable for large prints. However, most do not, and so this discussion focuses on the digital single lens reflex camera, which does include those professional features and more.

What Brand Should You Buy?

You should buy the brand that feels comfortable to you because there isn't a great deal of difference in the end results among all the major brands. Go to your local camera store and handle the equipment. Ergonomics is important; how does the Pentax, Canon, Nikon, Olympus, or Sony DSLR feel in your hands? Will you be comfortable with the location of the camera's controls? Another factor in determining which camera to buy might be lens availability. Maybe a relative has a good collection of lenses that you can use if you buy the DSLR that accommodates those lenses. Many photographers have made their purchase decisions based on this alone.

How Many Megapixels Do You Need?

The great megapixel war isn't over yet. Camera manufacturers keep pumping up and advertising those numbers with exclamation points in such a way as to make consumers think the number of megapixels is the most important technical specification to consider in purchasing their cameras. It's not. In fact, it was a relief to learn that the publisher of this book requires all digital images to be made with cameras with just six megapixels or more. That meant I was able to use images from one of my older DSLRs, and if I were so inclined, could even have used some images from a P&S camera I love so much. You would be hard pressed to find a DSLR camera today with less than ten megapixels. Cameras at the lowest end of today's megapixel landscape will produce brilliant photos capable of being printed to massive proportions and hung on your wall for all to enjoy.

What Lenses Do You Need?

Lens selection is very important to most photographers, and decisions about these selections must be made very carefully because lenses often cost more than the camera. Perhaps you already have a 35mm (film) SLR camera and you've heard that your lenses will work with modern DSLRs of the same brand. This is generally true, but can be very tricky. Often, in order to use an older lens on a modern camera, you will give up some important feature as a trade-off. For example, with some older lenses you might have to focus manually instead of using the camera's autofocus capability. You might even have to do

Drewry's Bluff in Chesterfield County is one of many locations along America's Founding River where visitors can see Civil War weapons that were used to defend Richmond from Union attack.

without in-camera exposure metering. Many photographers are comfortable with the trade-offs, but most would prefer to use all the capabilities of their cameras, which might require purchasing new lenses.

One of the biggest misconceptions about lenses among photographers is the idea that "more is better" when it comes to how much light a lens will allow to reach the camera's sensor (or film). Typically, the larger the aperture, the more light the lens will transmit. The numerical system by which apertures are measured—the lower the number, the larger the lens aperture—is confusing to many photographers. An f1.8 lens, for example, will transmit more light than an f2.8 lens. There is a trend among photographers today to want massive, light-gathering lenses (referred to as "fast" in the industry). They are massive because the more light a lens will transmit, the more glass is necessary, and that translates into size and weight. Fast lenses are necessary if you plan to shoot in dark venues such as concerts or other entertainment events, night street scenes, etc. But this discussion is about shooting landscapes in bright sunlight, so fast lenses are not necessary. Don't ever fall for the line that faster is better. Often, the opposite is true—lenses with smaller maximum apertures can produce extremely good quality images given enough light. A lens manufacturer might sacrifice image quality of a lens in order to make it a fast lens.

Most modern DSLRs come in some sort of kit, and the lenses included are often referred to as "kit" lenses. Some photographers prefer to scrap the kit lens in favor of fast lenses or lenses that have greater zoom range, wider angles, or greater telephoto capability. Many kits include two lenses so photographers will have extended shooting range right out of the box. If your kit comes with only one lens, it likely will be an 18-55 millimeter zoom, and it will not be a fast lens. Maximum aperture ranges for kit lenses will generally be about f3.5 at the wide-angle end to f5.6 at the longer (55mm) end.

The 18-55mm kit lens is probably all the lens you need to take great photos of rivers. You need a reasonably wide angle of coverage in order to get large portions of the river's beauty in the photo. The angle of coverage at 18mm in most modern DSLRs is seventy-six degrees. If you're thinking in terms of 35mm SLR cameras, the angle of coverage is equivalent to that of a 27mm lens. This is adequate coverage for most river scenes, and the maximum angle that was used for all of the photos in this book. (Angles of coverage in this discussion assume an APS-C or DX-size camera sensor. Some more expensive, professional DSLRs have full-frame sensors, and the angle of coverage on those cameras is approximately the same as on 35mm film cameras.) In addition, because you will be shooting in bright sunlight, a fast lens is not necessary. You should think in terms of smaller apertures instead of larger ones because smaller apertures increase your depth of field and overall sharpness.

Good Support Is Essential

A tripod is a must for good landscape photography. Most photographers have a steady enough hand to shoot at fast shutter speeds without a tripod, but the extra support it affords is well worth the effort required to transport it and set it up on location. Some digital cameras have vibration reduction or image stabilization features that eliminate some of the camera-motion blur associated with hand-held photos, but this is not a substitute for a solid camera support. If you choose to use a tripod for your landscape photos, consult your camera's user manual to see if you should switch off the electronic image stabilizer.

A monopod is a good substitute for a tripod in landscape photography. As the name implies, this camera support employs just one leg instead of three, and the contact with the ground is what gives added stability to the camera. In landscape photography you will often trudge through forests, jungles, rocky hills, or even swamps to get the photograph you desire. Carrying a tripod on such jaunts will add extra bulk and weight, and that might make it too awkward to be useful. In those cases, a monopod works fine and makes a great walking stick when not supporting your camera. The James River swallowed up my monopod in April 2010. Thank goodness a camera was not attached to it.

A monopod is a good substitute for a tripod for keeping a camera steady when shooting landscape photos. This self-portrait of author-photographer Will Daniel was taken using the self-timer of a camera on a tripod.

Lens Accessories

A good circular polarizing filter is a handy accessory for landscape photographers. It can turn drab colors into vibrant, deeply saturated tones. Because of the way your camera's digital sensor reacts to light, make sure your polarizing filter has the circular designation rather than linear. Also, when using a circular polarizer for landscape photography, always use the camera's daylight white balance setting. Your camera probably defaults to automatic white balance, which is great for most color shooting, but might negate the effects of the circular polarizer.

Most photographers like to use an ultraviolet or skylight filter simply to protect the lens. This is a good idea if the filter you buy is a good one, such as one that has multi-coating. Avoid cheap filters, as they can have a negative impact on your images, and don't use a protective filter in combination with a polarizer. A lens hood is another important accessory for outdoor photography. The hood prevents stray light rays from entering your camera causing flare patterns. Lens hoods generally do not come with a camera's kit lens, but can be purchased separately.

What Is ISO and Where Should You Set It?

ISO is short for International Organization of Standardization. In photography it relates to sensitivity to light, with the lower the ISO setting the more light required to take a photo, and vice versa. In digital photography, the user sets the ISO based on the lighting conditions. It can be changed at any time during the photography session if the light changes, or if fast action would require faster shutter speeds than what are attainable with lower ISO settings.

The higher the ISO, the more light is transmitted to the sensor of digital cameras, but higher ISOs involve trade-offs. In the digital world, high ISOs result in what is called noise, which is simply annoying artifacts in the image that detract from the image quality and make it nearly impossible to make large prints. In landscape photography, the lower the ISO the better. You will typically use ISO 100 or 200 for your bright-sun, blue-sky landscape images, and the quality will be superb compared to an ISO of say 1,200.

Finding Access Points

Don't trespass on private property. I may have trespassed a time or two in my zeal to capture the images in this book, but I never did so knowingly. Often, what appears to be a public road is actually on private property, but you don't know that because a "private property" sign may have been removed. In this case, you'll end up in someone's cornfield or perhaps violate a railroad's right-of-way.

When I first started shooting the James River, I used my computer map program to locate what looked like access points. My success rate using maps was only about fifty percent because so many of those mapped points were on private property. Whenever possible, ask the owner of the property if you can shoot there. Most will say yes if you're polite and respectful.

Using maps was good, but I needed to increase my success rate. So I started using Google Earth, a satellite-imaging program. I use a dual-monitor setup with my computer system, so I began opening my map program on one monitor and the corresponding satellite image on the other. Zooming in on a satellite image produces a reasonable basis for deciding whether the road ends at the river on private or public land. This method increased my success rate to about seventy-five percent. Your results, as they say, may vary.

Thank you for reading my book, and happy shooting.

Books

Calos, Mary Mitchell, Charlotte Easterling, and Ella Sue Rayburn. *Old City Point and Hopewell: The First 370 Years*. Norfolk, Virginia: The Donning Company/Publishers, 1983.

Garrison, Webb. *A Treasury of Virginia Tales*. Nashville, Tennessee: Rutledge Hill Press, Inc., 1991.

Nesbitt, Mark. *Rebel Rivers: A Guide to Civil War Sites on the Potomac, Rappahannock, York, and James*. Mechanicsburg, Pennsylvania: Stackpole Books, 1993.

Rouse, Parke, Jr. *The James: Where A Nation Begins*. Richmond, Virginia: Dietz Press, 1990.

Tyler-McGraw, Marie. *At the Falls: Richmond, Virginia, and Its People*. Chapel Hill, North Carolina: The University of North Carolina Press, 1994.

Winegar, Garvey. *The Unseen River*. Richmond, Virginia: Richmond Times-Dispatch, 1993.

Woodlief, Ann. *In River Time: The Way of the James*. Chapel Hill, North Carolina: Algonquin Books of Chapel Hill, 1985.

Magazine Articles

Firebaugh, Anita J. "Down Home in Eagle Rock," *Cooperative Living Magazine*, February 2000.
Hare, Judy. "Down Home in Smithfield," *Cooperative Living Magazine*, October 2000.

World Wide Web

American Civil War Center, The. http://www.tredegar.org

Captain John Smith Chesapeake National Historic Trail. http://www.virginia.org/johnsmithtrail

Chippokes Plantation State Park. http://www.dcr.virginia.gov/state_parks/chi.shtml

City of Lynchburg. http://www.lynchburgva.gov

City of Hampton. http://www.hampton.va.us/

Downtown Hampton. http://www.downtownhampton.com

Fort Pocahontas. http://www.fortpocahontas.org

Hatton Ferry. http://www.thehattonferry.org

James River Advisory Council. http://www.jamesriveradvisorycouncil.com

James River Association. http://www.jamesriverassociation.org

James River Park. http://www.jamesriverpark.org

James River Plantations. http://www.jamesriverplantations.org

Morrison, Col. E. M. *A Brief History of Isle of Wight County, Virginia*. http://www.rootsweb.ancestry.com/~vaisleof/history.htm

National Park Service, James River Plantations. http://www.nps.gov/nr/travel/jamesriver/wes.htm

Sherwood Forest Plantation. http://www.sherwoodforest.org

Smithfield and Isle of Wight Convention and Visitors Bureau. http://www.smithfield-virginia.com.

Surry County, Virginia. http://www.surrycountyva.gov

Virginia Department of Conservation and Recreation. http://www.dcr.virginia.gov, James River Heritage Trail

Virginia Department of Game and Inland Fisheries. http://www.dgif.virginia.gov

Virginia Institute of Marine Science. http://www.vims.edu/newsandevents/topstories/hampton_boat_study.php